TIME
OUT

Other books by Steve Case:

Hands-On Service Ideas for Youth (Pacific Press)
It's My Choice Junior Baptismal Guide, Student Workbook
It's My Choice Junior Baptismal Guide, Teacher's Manual
Shall We Dance? (La Sierra University Press)

To order, call 1-800-765-6955.
Visit us at www.reviewandherald.com for information on
other Review and Herald products.

steve case

TIME
OUT

Quick Devotions for Teens

Я

REVIEW AND HERALD® PUBLISHING ASSOCIATION
HAGERSTOWN, MD 21740

The author assumes full responsibility for the accuracy of all facts and quotations as cited in this book.

This book was
Edited by Andy Nash
Copyedited by Delma Miller and James Cavil
Cover designed by Saschane Stephenson
Interior designed by Tina M. Ivany
Page makeup by Tina M. Ivany
Cover art by AP Photo/Neil Brake: back cover; Corbis: crowd; PhotoDisc: stop watch and eyes

Typeset: Veljovic Book 12/14

PRINTED IN U.S.A.
05 04 03 02 01   5 4 3 2 1

R&H Cataloging Service
Case, Steve, 1957-
    Time out!

    1. Teenagers—Prayer books and devotions—English.   I. Title

                    242.63

ISBN 0-8280-1555-4

DEDICATION

Dedicated to my mom,

Billie Ann Case,

who modeled a consistent devotional life

and still always seems to be able to take time out for me.

CONTENTS

Relationships

Relationships
The Bottom Line

Some people won't trust God because they've never trusted anyone.

How can I have more friends? What does it take to get a true friend?

Take a moment to think about why you have the friends you do right now. What brought you together? What keeps you together? What's the bottom line when it comes to friends?

Is it money? Money can put you certain places and give you more impressive toys, but is that the bottom line for friendship? It can make somebody a sugar daddy by playing the role of a bank, but it can't be solid ground for true friends.

How about looks? Isn't it great to be attractive? And isn't it wonderful when others want to be around you because you're so good-looking? But beauty is in the eye of the beholder. What if the ones doing the beholding don't think you're good-looking? How a person looks might be an important starting point for some, but it's too superficial to be the bottom line for friendship.

What about someone who makes you a better person? Could that be the foundation of a good friendship? Actually, that sounds more like a coach than a friend. And while some coaches become friends, simply helping to make somebody better isn't enough to be the bedrock of friendship.

Maybe the secret is somebody always available to help. Everybody needs help, at least some of the time. Could that be the secret to being real friends? Actually, that's more of a criteria for being a servant or even a slave, not necessarily a friend.

Perhaps it all boils down to simple kindness—being nice, considerate, caring, doing positive things for the other person. Actually, that sounds more like being a good mom!

Probably the bottom line for all friendships is something obvious like love. Love is about as big as you can get, and friendship is a pretty big thing. But even if love is the "right answer," what is that love based on?

The bottom line for all friendships is trust. And typically trust develops over time and through lots of experiences. No wonder God seeks us in every situation—He wants our trust in Him to continue to grow. And no wonder true friends stick together through thick and thin—trust provides security. But trust is more than just going through a predictable routine. It involves appreciating and supporting each other, and being able to count on each other to do just that.

Some people won't trust God because they've never trusted anyone. Some people won't trust anyone because they don't trust God. Trust involves a certain amount of risk. And when someone trusts you, it opens the door for you to trust them in return—trust awakens trust.

Trust is like an intricately formed glass crystal—it takes lots of time and heat to develop, but it can be marred or destroyed in an instant. But because trust is the bottom line in friendship, only those willing to risk trusting will experience depth in their friendships.

With trust being so crucial, here are a few key questions regarding the bottom line in all friendships. In what specific areas do you trust God right now? Where would you like to trust Him more? Whom do you trust more—your friends or God? Why? Are you more apt to take the initiative in trusting others, or do you let them trust you before you trust them? What has influenced you to trust or not to trust God? What makes you trustworthy?

Trust in the Lord with all your heart . . . and he will make your paths straight.
Proverbs 3:5, 6, NIV.

Starting Point

What's your starting point?

Frequently people talk about how important a person's *direction* in life can be. Obviously your direction will determine where you're going and what you'll pass along the way.

But there's something every bit as important as your direction, and that's your starting point. In fact, your *starting point* may change the direction you really want to go.

Let me illustrate. If you're taking a trip by car and you have 1,000 miles to go, due east, you'll not only want to head east, but you'll need to take provision for getting fuel along the way—probably for yourself as well as your vehicle.

If you have only 10 miles to go, you'll still head the same direction, east, but your starting point is so close that you probably wouldn't have much concern about fuel or any other provisions.

What if your starting point was 500 miles east of your destination? Yes, it's a different starting point, east of your destination, so you'll need to head west. With a starting point like that, you'd actually *change your direction* and head west, the opposite direction! And with 500 miles to go, you had better make more plans than just hopping in a car and driving 15 minutes.

I could ask what direction you're heading in your relationship with God, but first I should probably ask what your starting point is. Once we figure that out, we can make a better choice about what direction would be best. Your starting point has to do with all kinds of input you've already received, which influences where you see yourself right now.

For example, if your image of a father is negative, your

starting point in reference to God being like a father probably is negative, unless you've already substituted a positive
image of God in place of your negative father image. If your
image of a father is positive, it's likely that your starting
point for God being like a father probably is positive.

For many of us, our starting point for life as a whole
often leaves us feeling very inadequate. We seem to be sur-
rounded by people who *have* more and *are* more than us—it
can be depressing. The typical advertising plot is designed to
make you feel like something is missing from your life . . .
but if you'll just buy Hog's Breath toothpaste, you'll quickly
become the world's most potent magnet for the opposite
sex. You're a mess, but if you use Wipe 'em Up towelettes,
your family will be happy and all of you will go on a wonderful vacation together. If you drink Dragon High Life beer,
you'll be funny, witty, have lots of friends, and shoot pool
better than anyone else.

Here are four individuals or groups we relate to. Which
one do you relate to first, which one second, and so on?

A. The world I live in

B. Friends and family

C. Myself

D. God

If your starting point is A, you run the risk of taking the
following path. The world (A) is a mean and tough place,
and it keeps bombarding me with messages that I'm not
good enough. In fact, my friends and family (B) let me know
when I don't measure up as well. Nobody likes me, and
frankly, I don't like myself, either (C). And even though people say otherwise, I seriously doubt if God likes me (D).

What a destructive cycle! Even though it ends with God,

it was a bad starting point, which results in a bad direction. Let's reverse the order by making God the starting point.

D. God

C. Myself

B. Friends and family

A. The world I live in

How does God (D) relate to me? God made me, died for me, is intimately interested in my life. Hey, that's a great start! If God likes me, you know what—I'll like me (C) too. And with God thinking so highly of me and since I now have some God-confidence, I can relate to my friends and family (B) in positive ways, regardless of how they relate to me. In fact, I will love people in the community and around the world (A), including those I don't even know yet, because my starting point is what God thinks of me.*

Your starting point makes all the difference in the world when it comes to your direction and where you end up. Do you start with what the world thinks of you or what God thinks of you? What's your starting point?

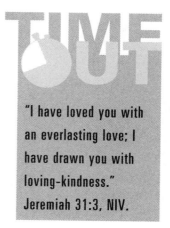

"I have loved you with an everlasting love; I have drawn you with loving-kindness."
Jeremiah 31:3, NIV.

How to Have More Friends Than You Know What to Do With

Listen to what others say instead of doing all the talking yourself.

I guarantee: YOU CAN HAVE MORE FRIENDS THAN YOU KNOW WHAT TO DO WITH IF YOU JUST FOLLOW THE FOUR STEPS I'M ABOUT TO SHARE WITH YOU. Most people don't believe it. And most people don't do it either. That's why so many people will want to be friends with you—because hardly anybody else is doing this.

Step 1: *Get the history on the person.* Just ask some simple questions, such as "Where do you go to school?" or "What do you do when you hang out?" or "Is there any particular reason you keep that duckbilled platypus in your pocket?"

Everybody knows that you have to find out about a person before you can really become friends. First impressions are worth something, but unless you find out more about people, they will merely be imaginary friends. You can find out more "history" about a person by just being around them, by asking questions, observing, or checking out other info sources. Most people get to step 1, but they never get to step 2.

Step 2: *Give 'em a high five!* No, it isn't limited to a literal "high five." It just means some type of positive feedback, you know—affirmation. But however you choose to communicate it, the compliment is based on something about that person (their "history"), such as "You sure have some quick moves on

What specific things can I do to move to the next step in my relationships?

the court" or "You totally aced that test—got any tips for this under-achiever?" or "Retro bell-bottoms—now, that's what I call styling."

There's no need to kiss up to people, but if you aren't accustomed to giving positive feedback, it might be a little awkward at first. If you can't come up with anything positive about a person, find out more history until you discover something.

> A man that hath friends must shew himself friendly: and there is a friend that sticketh closer than a brother.
> Proverbs 18:24.

We all crave positive feedback, yet most relationships never make it to the second stage because so few people give compliments. One of the best ways to give a "high five" is to listen to what others say instead of doing all of the talking yourself. Talk about what's interesting to them first, and then be ready to share something about yourself once they're ready to listen. When people feel that you're really listening to them, they're apt to share deeper history about themselves. When you keep giving "high fives" they're apt to keep sharing more. That develops trust, which is what makes friendships special.

Step 3: *Help, I need you!* We all need help in various parts of our lives. But we probably won't admit it unless there's a person we can trust—somebody who has given us plenty of "high fives" in the past. When you've gone beyond simply being nice (high fives) to the point of really needing somebody else, you begin to share your soul with that person. That's very risky, and that's why it usually won't happen until there has been loads of affirmation.

Step 4: *Best friends.* This won't happen until you've invested in each other and can share things with each other that you wouldn't share with just anyone. Even after you're apart for a while, you can pick up right where you left off because the trust keeps the relationship secure.

When you continue to give high fives, you're likely to find lots of people who will invest in a relationship with you to the point of asking for your help—and offering their own help to you. That's when you'll have to make some hard decisions, because you won't be able to be on a deep friendship level with everyone who will want to be friends with you.

Seeing the Invisible

See anyone with a need? That person is Jesus to you right now.

It doesn't take much for some people to give up on God. Maybe it's breaking up with a boyfriend or girlfriend during junior high. It could be that temporary but intense moment when you found out you didn't make the team, or when the pastor didn't notice you that one day.

For some people, it's a big event, such as the death of a family member or friend; some devastation, called an "act of God"; or being overwhelmed by tragedies, evil, or suffering on this planet. The question forms in your mind: "Is there a God?" Or "If there is a God, where is He?" While some deny the existence of God, others simply admit they have no evidence. They may be open to the reality of God, but God seems to be invisible.

How do you respond to a request to see the invisible God? Do you speak of some personal experience that internally has meaning for you, but might be explained by others as nothing more than a good upbringing or a vivid experience on the road toward emotional maturity?

Let me suggest two places to look for the invisible God. These are very tangible and observable, but they require a unique perspective.

The first place to see the invisible God is in people who reach out and meet another person's need. It could be the obvious things, such as feeding the homeless at a soup kitchen or distributing clothes or blankets to the needy. It could be less conspicuous, such as donating blood, cleaning up a park, playing with children, listening to an old-timer. You might see God when

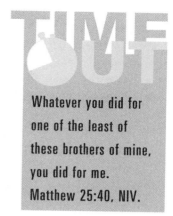

Whatever you did for one of the least of these brothers of mine, you did for me. Matthew 25:40, NIV.

one teen comforts another or a supportive adult shows up to watch you in that school-sponsored event.

If you need more of a clue on where to look for Jesus, try reading the stories of Jesus in Matthew, Mark, Luke, and John. In several settings and in a variety of ways, Jesus made it clear that His followers would do the same types of things He had been doing (see John 14:12-14; John 15:12-17; John 17:22-26). In fact, the promise of the Holy Spirit, who would come and live within the believers, was not just for personal edification. Those filled would live a spiritual life that would make it obvious that there is a God (see Matthew 5:16).

Try this out today: Look for examples of people who are continuing the ministry that Jesus started. Look for people who reach out and meet the needs of others. When you do that, Jesus will no longer be invisible.

But there's a second place to see Jesus. In a sense, it's the flip side of the first way of seeing Him. Whenever and wherever you see somebody with a need, you're seeing Jesus. That's right! The AIDS victim, the alcoholic, the prostitute, the self-righteous, the poor, the liar, the haggard parent, the worried child, the stressed-out teen, the burned-out teacher, the callused lawyer, the lonely bar hopper, the pastor who's just going through the motions.

Would you really like to see Jesus today? You can! But it necessitates a different view of reality. Do you see anyone with a need? That person is Jesus to you right now. Or have you forgotten the very words of Jesus in Matthew 25:40: "When you help someone in need, you are really helping Me!"

But like the people in Jesus' day, we want to see power and glory. We want a superman! And so an obvious Jesus repeatedly gets passed by because He's invisible in contrast to what we're looking for.

Would you like to see the invisible Jesus? You probably have, but didn't know it. Open your eyes. Wherever you see someone in need and whenever you see somebody responding to a need, you see the invisible Jesus.

At the end of today, finish this sentence: "I saw Jesus today when . . ."

---

*This reversal comes from Bruce Larson, *No Longer Strangers* (Waco, Tex.: Word Books, 1971).

Spirituality

"In" and "Out"

What's the inner core of who you are?

What do the following things have in common?

1. Walking barefoot on the beach
2. Attending church
3. Having sex with your spouse
4. Going to a great concert
5. Meditating

Can you pick out the golden thread running through all five of these activities?

Try again!

You mean it isn't obvious to you?

Give up? OK, each of these has been called a "spiritual" experience. Get it?

I don't! I've experienced all five, but I wouldn't name the common denominator "spirituality." It makes me wonder what people mean when they use the word "spiritual."

Usually the word "religion" gets used in contrast to "spiritual." For example, religion is formal, dead, going-through-the-motions, do's and don'ts, and takes place in a cold and damp building, boring, and meaningless. But spirituality is spontaneous, alive, unique, personal, liberating, whenever

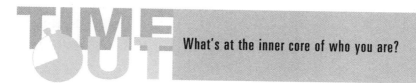

What's at the inner core of who you are?

and wherever you want, captivating, and deep!

Based on those adjectives alone, I'm all for spirituality. Who wouldn't be? It's obvious that spirituality is the hot thing and religion is a total dud. Even pop icons, such as Madonna, Brad Pitt, and Deion Sanders are into the spiritual.

When I press people on what they mean by "spiritual," they offer some kind of gibberish like "It's so deep and experiential that it transcends nomenclature as its effervescence emanates from my inner consciousness in search of the wings of a dove." Let me translate: "I really have no idea what I'm talking about, but there's something very emotional happening to me and I don't know what to call it, so I'm calling it 'spiritual.'"

Hey, I'm into things that are deep and meaningful. I'm just not sure these people are accurate in their word selection. It seems that they're describing something at the very core of their being, which shouldn't be treated lightly. But their inner search falls short of being truly spiritual. It's internal, but unless it latches onto God, it's only a cheap imitation of what is truly spiritual. What a tragedy if they bypassed institutional religion for a personal but phony substitute for God. If this is what's "in," then count me out.

> What happened was this: People knew God perfectly well, but when they didn't treat him like God, refusing to worship him, they trivialized themselves into silliness and confusion so that there was neither sense nor direction left in their lives. They pretended to know it all, but were illiterate regarding life. They traded the glory of God who holds the whole world in his hands for cheap figurines you can buy at any roadside stand. Romans 1:21-23, Message.

Getting to God

We already have God's attention.

When it comes to the interplay between males and females, getting the other person's attention has to be the first step. But what if you get the other person's attention and they aren't the least bit interested? What if they're repulsed? No wonder we develop all kinds of sly ways to get somebody's attention, and yet act like we really aren't . . . until they give an encouraging response.

When couples are asked who made the first step to initiate a relationship, most males claim that they did. But videotaped observation reveals that more females make the first move. The males might have been vaguely aware of something, but what they thought was the first move was only their response to the initial move made by the female. Could that really be true?

How does it work in our relationship with God? What does it take to get God's attention? If we live a basically decent life, would that do it? Or do we have to live a really good life? Is attending church a necessity? Does leading out in church activities boost our chances? Do you think God would zero in on you more if you went forward during an altar call and made some kind of public commitment to Him? What if you said you'd become a pastor? If you were super-faithful in personal devotions, would that do the trick?

How about community service? If we get school credit for it, could we just trade that in for heavenly credit? If you ignored your sibling's annoyances, would it make God look your way? How about if you just went along with what your parents said instead of challenging them?

Perhaps, instead of trying to do specific good deeds, it's more a matter of generally following the golden rule: treat others the way you want to be treated (Matthew 7:12). Maybe the most effective attention-getting method would be to try out Micah 6:8: "He has shown you, O man, what is good; and what does the Lord require of you; but to *do justly,* to *love mercy,* and to *walk humbly with your God?*" (NKJV). What does it really take to get God's attention?

The basis of all pagan religion is that we can do something to get God's attention. For eons people have tried all sorts of ways to get God to notice them—walking on hot coals, sacrificing children on an altar, cutting one's self in hopes that the blood would provoke notice, fasting and praying, giving to the poor, going through the motions of religious duties.

Out of all the world's religions, Christianity stands out quite distinctly from the rest when it comes to getting God's attention. *The basis of Christianity is that we already have God's attention.* Here are a few examples:

"We love because he first loved us" (1 John 4:19, NIV).

"Surely I am with you always, to the very end of the age" (Matthew 28:20, NIV).

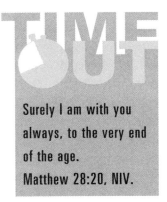

Surely I am with you always, to the very end of the age.
Matthew 28:20, NIV.

"God showed his great love for us by sending Christ to die for us while we were still sinners" (Romans 5:8, NLT).

So if you've been trying to get God's attention, give it up! The One who has His eyes on the sparrows (see Matthew 10:29-31) certainly has His eyes on you. Whether you know it or not—whether you think you started it or not—He's got you covered.

3 Talking (and Listening)

Here, try it for yourself.

Don't you just hate it when somebody talks to you and then when you respond, they don't even listen at all? How rude!

That's almost as bad as when you talk to somebody and then they say absolutely nothing in return. It's like "Hello? Were you even listening?"

Is that how prayer works (or doesn't work) with you? Do you talk to God and then get no response at all? Or do you talk to God and then not even listen for a response?

For years I've felt guilty about not listening for the voice of God during or following my prayers. When I tried to listen, all I heard was silence. When others prodded me to listen for that "still small voice," it seemed that my own rambling thoughts carried me off the topic at hand. When others told me to go with that thought because God was leading me, we eventually ended up with thoughts that I really don't think God wanted me to think about, especially after I had surrendered those thoughts to Him.

I don't doubt that others get impressions or even hear an audible voice from God. But it hasn't worked very well for me. I've tried the ACTS prayer: adoration, confession, thanksgiving, and supplication. I've tried journaling, praying out loud, having prayer partners, and more.

My breakthrough came when I read the Psalms as prayers. The pedantic lines I learned as a child, such as praying for God to "bless the missionaries and colporteurs across the seas," I traded for the words of an earlier artist—David. And by using a modern paraphrase like Eugene

Peterson's *The Message,* my prayers changed from ritual to communion. Finally my imagination took a phrase, a sentence, a paragraph. God spoke to me, and I responded. Here are a few examples:

"God rules: there's something to shout over!" (Psalm 97:1, Message). I get really excited about sports, especially championships or finals. Yep, I start shouting. But it's only a game. What about the things that count the most to me? What could I shout or cheer about there? Oh yes, Yahweh rules! That's something to shout about. Let's continue.

"Anyone can see that the brightest and best die, wiped out right along with fools and dunces. They leave all their prowess behind, move into their new home, The Coffin, the cemetery their permanent address. And to think they named counties after themselves!" (Psalm 49:10, 11, Message).

"This is what happens to those who live for the moment, who only look out for themselves: Death herds them like sheep straight to hell" (verses 13, 14, Message).

Wow, that's harsh stuff! But it's sort of true—well, I guess it's just plain true. We all die. Some get there faster than others. It kind of makes me wonder what life's all about.

Here, try it for yourself. As you listen to the next few lines from God, respond yourself. Ready? Here it goes:

"So don't be impressed with those who get rich and pile up

My choice is you, God, first and only. And now I find I'm your choice! . . . I'm happy from the inside out, and from the outside in, I'm firmly formed. You canceled my ticket to hell—that's not my destination! Ever since you took my hand, I'm on the right way. Psalm 16:5-11, Message.

fame and fortune. They can't take it with them; fame and fortune all get left behind. Just when they think they've arrived and folks praise them because they've made good, they enter the family burial plot where they'll never see sunshine again. We aren't immortal. We don't last long. Like our dogs, we age and weaken. And die" (verses 16-20, Message).

Let's try another one. Listen and then talk in response to this:

"My choice is you, God, first and only. And now I find I'm *your* choice! . . . I'm happy from the inside out, and from the outside in, I'm firmly formed. You canceled my ticket to hell—that's not my destination! . . . Ever since you took my hand, I'm on the right way" (Psalm 16:5-11).

Keep talking . . . and listening . . . and talking . . . and listening.

 **How Prayer Changes You**

If you're a control freak, the antidote is prayer.

Some people see prayer as a science—with a cause-and-effect relationship, a series of asking dappled with some thanksgiving and praise, somehow intensified by increasing the number of people praying or by praying for a long period of time. If you can just figure out the equation, prayer works!

Others view prayer more like art—a personal expression from one's soul with a definite listening component. Intensity gets measured as quality rather than as quantity. Instead of accurately giving equal time to asking and thanking, you simply purge your heart and take in a fresh, gurgling spring.

Beyond the tension and blend of prayer being a science

Pour out your hearts to him, for God is our refuge. Psalm 62:8, NIV.

and art, prayer also makes its own impact on the person who prays. Because prayer brings people and events through the consciousness of the person praying, prayer changes the person praying. You find yourself more involved and interested in the things and people who come to mind during your seasons of prayer.

This works even when you pray for people you don't like. Read Psalm 69 or Psalm 109 for some strong words from David regarding his enemies, followed by a request for God's kindness to be given to David. Instead of letting his anger fester inside himself, and instead of getting it off his chest by dumping on his enemies, David pours it out to God. This frees him of the pressure he has been feeling, and does so without the potential reaction from his enemies if he simply dumped his feelings on them. God is big enough to handle it, so prayer can purge the internal negative and destructive elements for the person who prays. Jeremiah found relief in this way also (see Jeremiah 19; 20).

Prayer frees the one praying from the clutches of the past because it accesses forgiveness. It also chases away the anxieties regarding the future, because all things are placed into God's hands. The person who prays can live the present moment to its fullest, free of the guilt from the past and free from the anxiety about the future. So if you're a control freak, the antidote is prayer. Put things in God's hands.

Here's a great way to put this in practice in your own life. Over time, read through the Psalms as prayers. As you read, note whether the psalm is a prayer of praise to God, a call for help, a venting of anger, a song of thanksgiving— feel free to come up with your own classification. You can use color coding or just write in your Bible. Develop a listing of praise psalms, anger-purging psalms, etc., so you can turn right to some of the options in the future instead of blindly thumbing through Scripture when in need.

Yes, prayer reaches heaven. But it instantly begins to make a difference here on earth, including how it affects the person who does the praying. Are you ready to be changed by your own prayers?

Bible

Missing the Boat

The purpose of the Bible is to get us with Jesus.

You just don't get it, do you?"

Have you ever said that? Has anyone ever said it to you? Have you felt it? It's pathetic, frustrating, bewildering, unfortunate, enough to make you want to quit.

One time Jesus said it to the Pharisees. You see, they took great pride in knowing the Bible, and yet they didn't get it—they didn't realize that the Bible is all about Jesus. Jesus, the Son of God, was standing right in front of them, and they thought He was more like the devil than like God. They didn't get it.

Here's how Jesus put it: "You're constantly studying the Scriptures, and you think that by doing so you have eternal life, but these same Scriptures talk about me. You refuse to believe who I am, so there's no chance that you will ever receive eternal life" (John 5:39, 40, Clear Word).

Unbelievable! Studying Scripture and not even recognizing God when He shows up on your doorstep. Talk about missing the boat. That's about as bad as:

riding an exercise bike to lose weight, but eating candy bars for energy and drinking milk shakes to cool down;

putting someone down because you think your clever, sharp tongue will make them want to be around you more;

feasting once a week by attending church, but starving the rest of the week by neglecting personal time with God;

riding a motorcycle in cutoffs and a tank top, but remembering to strap your helmet to the back bar;

using a condom for "safe sex," even though the HIV virus can penetrate the condom more easily than a tricycle enter-

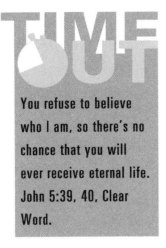

You refuse to believe who I am, so there's no chance that you will ever receive eternal life. John 5:39, 40, Clear Word.

ing a three-car garage;

staying up all night to study so you'll do better on a test;

spending money on somebody to show you care, even though all they really want is your time;

dropping off your children at church but not attending yourself;

blowing away brain cells with drugs so you can be more enlightened;

buying something you'll never use, but figuring you've saved money because you bought it on sale;

making a new commitment to be sexually pure but then placing yourself in the same kinds of compromising situations that broke your commitment before;

attending school regularly but sleeping through class;

trying to find quality friends, but spending more of your time and energy trying to look attractive on the outside instead of on the inside;

searching the Bible to be saved, but rejecting the Saviour revealed in the Bible;

wanting to be with Jesus, but spending no time in Scripture.

Are you getting it? The purpose of the Bible is to get us with Jesus. If you're ending up someplace else, you may need help discovering the Jesus of the Bible. If you want to get with Jesus and you aren't into Scripture, get with it. There's no need to miss the boat!

What Do You Expect?

What do you expect?

Just one look, and the thought races through your mind: *This must be the scrawniest guy I've ever seen in my entire life. How wimpy can you get?* Then he begins singing and you feel yourself being startled like so many have been. *That has to be the richest, fullest, bass voice since, well, ever!*

What did you expect?

He arrives in a new limousine with a full entourage following. Dressed impeccably, he steps out of the limo and strides toward the plush business complex. But as the police restrain the crowd, he suddenly pauses. Something has caught his eye. It's not another "important" person, nor is it a photo-op moment with a street urchin. He calls *you* by name. He remembers you from elementary school! You can hardly believe that he even picked you out of the crowd. He greets you and then jokes about the mud pies you used to make together by the swing set when you were in kindergarten. Others seem impatient that he stopped, especially since you're about as average as they come.

What did you expect?

She approaches, wearing a low V-neck top that's slightly tighter than, well, skintight. Her long blond hair probably isn't natural, but who knows for sure? Her skirt, or whatever that thin strip of cloth might be called, catches any eye that might have missed the upper half. When you finally find her face, it makes you say "Wow!" as well.

She pulls you aside, looks you directly in the eye, and states, "Nobody takes me seriously. Would you be my friend—someone I can confide in, someone who will join me

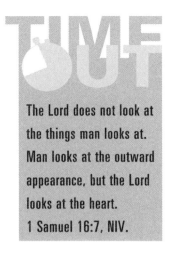

The Lord does not look at the things man looks at. Man looks at the outward appearance, but the Lord looks at the heart.
1 Samuel 16:7, NIV.

in grappling with issues far beyond the superficial and mundane topics everyone seems content to talk about? Will you?"

What did you expect?

It would be great to get a word from God. So you go to church—seems as good a place as any. You ask the senior pastor for counsel from God about an important matter. What he shares with you sounds more like the opinion he's formed over the years than a fresh word from the Lord. But an 8-year-old boy interjects by saying, "I received a message from the Lord last night, and He told me you would be here today."

What did you expect?

As you get older you learn what to expect. You've seen enough scrawny guys, rich guys, outward-appearance-only people and enough pastors to have some clear expectations. What are your expectations? Watch out!

Who would have expected the little boy Samuel to receive messages from God instead of the high priest, Eli? But God isn't limited by what we expect. And even though Samuel experienced this firsthand, his expectations got challenged as well.

For example, you're looking for a king. Would you check out the boy shepherds?

You want a soldier who can outwrestle a giant? Would you even consider the boy who bags the groceries?

You're trying to locate the prince's best friend. Does it make any sense to look for him hiding in a cave fearing for his life?

Someone has committed a double felony: murder and adultery. Would your first suspect be the king, who already has everything he could ever want?

The answer to the previous four characters is David. The first time he gets mentioned in Scripture is when God remonstrated Samuel by saying, "Man looks at the outward appearance, but the Lord looks on the heart." God still looks on the heart. And we humans continue to look at the outward appearance. It's what makes the first impression. What do you expect?

Do you spend more time at the start of your day getting your outward appearance ready or getting your heart ready? Are you more apt to comment on a person's outward appearance or their heart?

We deplore all the media attention given to superficial things, yet most of us dedicate more of our time and money to the outward appearance than to our soul.

What do you expect?

Not a Laughing Matter

No wonder Jesus wept.

As kids this was the first text we'd choose if we had to recite something from Scripture. Whoever went first always said "Jesus wept" because it was the easiest—the shortest verse in the whole Bible. (For some reason the brief verses "Rejoice evermore" and "Pray without ceasing" in

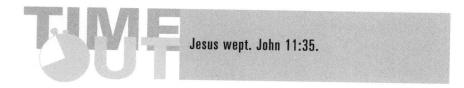

Jesus wept. John 11:35.

What causes you to weep today?

1 Thessalonians 5:16, 17 never stuck in our minds as short verses—only "Jesus wept.")

And everybody would laugh because the first person was clever enough to say the shortest verse. We didn't think of crying because Jesus cried; we simply wanted to complete the task of reciting a text.

We also used "Jesus wept" when taking any regular game and making it a "Sabbath game." Want to play tag on Sabbath? Just say "Jesus wept" when you get tagged, and then you can go free. And everybody would laugh again. We all knew "Jesus wept," but it didn't seem to elicit much more than a laugh from us.

Most of us didn't even know that our favorite verse came from the familiar story of Jesus' raising Lazarus from the dead. But it was only a matter of time until we would attend a funeral and discover that lots of people cry when someone has died. It would be several more years until we would make the connection that when Jesus wept at the graveside of Lazarus, God identified with human loss and heartache through personal experience.

But Jesus reversed that loss by raising Lazarus from the dead. Jesus wept because He knew that the incredible miracle He was about to perform still wouldn't lead some of the hard-hearted leaders to believe in Him (see John 11:37, 46, 53). And so Jesus wept.

Tragically, even though Jesus raised Lazarus from the grave, the religious leaders plotted to kill not only Jesus, the life-giver, but also Lazarus, the one who had been brought back from the dead (see John 11:53 and John 12:10). No wonder Jesus wept.

But this outright rejection in the face of overwhelming evidence has been played out over the centuries. Although some would call it unbelievable, the masses throughout time have chosen either to ignore or to spurn the life God offers them, some even seeking to deprive others of that life. Seeing the rejection of eternal life by so many over the expanse of earth's history, Jesus wept.

And so the shortest verse in the Bible depicts the longest agony of God. Jesus wept. It's certainly not a laughing matter.

 ## Flabby Muscles

"You ain't seen nothing yet! Suck it up, you big baby!"

It's possible to have nicely shaped muscles and still be weak. It's also possible to have great muscles and super strength, and then lose it all simply by failing to continue to work out.

And while everyone has muscles, some have only flabby muscles. These muscles still work. They just don't work as well as toned muscles would. As Hans and Franz have said: "You're just a girlie-man. We are here to (thump, thump) pump you up!"

For many situations, flabby muscles make absolutely no difference at all. For example, how well-toned do you need to be in order to sleep at night, or to drive a car (especially with power steering), or to brush your teeth, or to walk from the sofa to the refrigerator and back (all during one commercial break), or to listen to music, or to talk on the phone?

What difference does it make? It makes a difference only when you *need* well-toned muscles. That's why individuals (especially athletes) work out with weights. It's why sports teams go through drills and practices. It's the reason military personnel go through boot camp and maneuvers.

The book of Proverbs puts it this way: "If you are weak in a crisis, you are weak indeed" (Proverbs 24:10, TEV).

Is Christianity an invitation to flabby muscles or well-toned ones? Are we trying to mooch off of someone else's work, much like a boxer's entourage follows him in hopes of scavenging some of the excess after his paycheck arrives?

For some reason Christians often complain about the hardship they endure. What do they expect—that Christianity will be easy street? Here's how God answered Jeremiah's complaint of getting too much of a workout: "If you get tired racing against people, how can you race against horses? If you can't even stand up in the open country, how will you manage in the jungle by the Jordan?" (Jeremiah 12:5, TEV). Here's my rough paraphrase: "You ain't seen nothing yet! Suck it up, you big baby!"

I'm not trying to make God out to be a mean drill sergeant. Actually, God attempts to prepare us for tough times by providing practice and then graduating us to more challenging situations. In Matthew 25 Jesus tells two servants, "Well done, my good and faithful servant. You have been faithful in handling this small amount, so now I will give you many more responsibilities. Let's celebrate together!" (Matthew 25:21 NLT; repeated in verse 23). It can make you wonder what God is preparing you for when you face tough times now!

The first three chapters of Daniel recount three stories in which Shadrach, Meshach, and Abednego go through three increasingly challenging scenarios. We can only imagine what prepared them for these crises before they ever got to Babylon. In Daniel 1 they are faced with eating the food from the king's table, meat that had been offered to pagan gods.

If you are weak in a crisis, you are weak indeed.
Proverbs 24:10, TEV.

Along with Daniel, these three stood against the majority and received what appears to be both physical and supernatural rewards. In addition, they were being prepared for even bigger challenges.

In Daniel 2 the three Hebrews receive a death warrant that gets put off while they pray for a message from God to recall Nebuchadnezzar's dream and to discover its interpretation. Although all four pray, only Daniel receives the vision that spares their lives.

In Daniel 3 the three friends face a test without Daniel. Once again they receive the death decree because they didn't comply with the king's whims or plans. It makes you wonder if they sort of thought to themselves, *Here we go again—been there, done that,* when the king ordered them to be killed. Of all the Hebrew captives being trained in Babylon at that time, only these three were without flabby muscles when it came time to stand for God.

What about you? For what are you being prepared and groomed? Being a Christian in no way guarantees that life will be easy. In fact, you can expect just the opposite. So suck it up, because you're going to face some tough times. But you already saw that coming, didn't you?

Personal Growth

1 Crashing Without Burning

What do I have to lose?

The fear of failure paralyzes many. Most of us cop out of activities simply because we don't want to take the risk of failing. We may silently tell ourselves, "I may not succeed, but at least I won't fail."

This attitude shows itself in things like:

I won't take physics, because it might hurt my GPA.

I'm not going out for the basketball team, because I might get cut.

I won't attempt to develop that friendship, because I might get spurned.

Don't expect me to audition for the school play. What would I do if they gave the part to someone else instead of me?

There's no way I'll run for student office. Can you imagine putting up all those posters, giving a speech in front of everyone, and then losing?

I'm not going to try Christianity. It would probably last only a little while. This way I'll never be a hypocrite.

These paralysis producers can be prevented or overcome. Perhaps the core question to ask oneself is "What do I have to lose?" It might be one's reputation, dignity, friends, grades, future, security. The reality of losing any of these precious things might be real or might actually be a mirage, but the fear is certainly real.

Here's the key: failure doesn't have to be fatal.

In Proverbs 24:16 we read, "No matter how often honest people fall, they always get up again; but disaster destroys the wicked" (TEV). Honest, godly people fail. But they get back

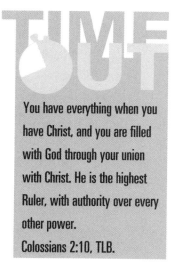

up again. Let's not deny it—it hurts to fall, it hurts to fail. But the righteous get back up. Why? What makes the difference?

"You have everything when you have Christ, and you are filled with God through your union with Christ. He is the highest Ruler, with authority over every other power" (Colossians 2:10, TLB). That's the difference! As Christians we're secure in our union with Christ and therefore have the most important thing. And because we do, we can take risks with the smaller things. Apart from Christ, we have little choice but to hover in fear and try to hold on to the little we have.

In the book of Romans Paul wrote, "When you were slaves of sin you didn't bother much with goodness. And what was the result? Evidently not good, since you are ashamed now even to think about those things you used to do, for all of them end in eternal doom. But now you are free from the power of sin and are slaves of God, and his benefits to you include holiness and everlasting life" (Romans 6:20-22, TLB).

Christians are free from the slavery of sin and selfishness controlling them. They're free to live for others and to take risks they would have never dreamed of before. Because of the security based on Christ, we have no need to fear failure because it never needs to be fatal.

Jesus certainly appeared to have crashed *and* burned when he died on the cross. He died in the most disgraceful manner known at that time. One of His own disciples turned Him in. The rest of His disciples left Him and even denied Him. Failure? It certainly seemed like it at the moment. But the Crucifixion was far from fatal, because Jesus is alive again. Failure (or seeming failure) never needs to be fatal, because we have everything when we have Christ.

Those willing to fail sometimes do. But oddly enough, they are also the only ones who succeed.

Don't Put Up With Put-downs

The antidote is usually to respond with affirmation.

I grew up with three sisters but no brothers. One of our family commandments was no hitting. So we didn't have fist-fights. But we more than made up for it by slicing and dicing each other with our words. I got so good at put-downs that nobody at home or at school even wanted to be around me. It proved to be a rather hollow success.

Strangely, I was proud of my skill. Looking back, I regret developing that well-rehearsed habit. I no longer want to use put-downs on others. In the Bible we read, "Encourage each other to build each other up, just as you are already doing" (1 Thessalonians 5:11, TLB). That's how I want to live now.

I've met others who also take a twisted pride in their ability to put down others. Some call it "capping" on another person. Occasionally I've noticed that others retaliate with their own put-down (a very natural reaction), and the war is on—a contest to see who can outwit and outdo the other. The tone of such an encounter is tense. When a person with a reputation for delving out put-downs shows up, notice how the conversation becomes guarded and people tense up. How pathetic!

Underneath put-downs is a sense of inadequacy and/or inferiority. It's an attempt to pull another person down to the level of the person who feels inferior. It's almost as if the per-

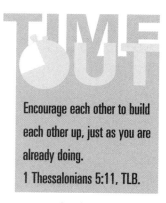

Encourage each other to build each other up, just as you are already doing.

1 Thessalonians 5:11, TLB.

son is trying to say, "I feel very inadequate when I compare myself to you. Let me try to make you appear worse than you are, then maybe others will think you are as bad as I am."

Those who artistically use put-downs on others have a core need to feel the security of complete acceptance by God. Once they embrace that, they can accept themselves and won't feel so inadequate as to compare themselves to others.

Does this apply to you? How often do you employ put-downs? Do others cringe when they're around you? Do you find yourself using put-downs when others show up, especially if they seem to be more talented in some area(s) than you? Do you need to bask in God's full acceptance of yourself to the point that you can feel secure regardless of who else happens to be around?

If you're the target for a striking viper of put-downs, the antidote is usually to respond with affirmation. When Paul quotes the proverb of heaping burning coals on the head of your enemy (Proverbs 25:21, 22), he concludes by writing, "Do not be overcome by evil, but overcome evil with good" (Romans 12:21, NIV).

The motivation for returning put-downs with affirmation isn't based on the person giving the put-downs. It's based on treating others the way God has treated you. God certainly has enough information to put us way down. But here's how He treats us instead: "The Lord is compassionate and gracious, slow to anger, abounding in love. He will not always accuse, nor will he harbor his anger forever; he does not treat us as our sins deserve or repay us according to our iniquities. For as high as the heavens are above the earth, so great is his love for those who fear him; as far as the east is from the west, so far has he removed our transgressions from us. As a father has compassion on his children, so the Lord has compassion on those who fear him; for he knows how we are formed, he remembers that we are dust" (Psalm 103:8-14, NIV).

When you return a put-down with an affirmation, it removes the sting and retaliation from the interchange; and it can support the person who obviously feels inferior. But be sure your tone of voice also communicates affirmation, since it's possible to use positive words in a sarcastic or cynical manner.

If a person uses a put-down to describe how you look, there's no need to agree or even to ignore the comment. Return it with a sincere affirmation, such as "Your hair always looks fabulous. What's your secret?"

When a person caps on something you said by purposely misinterpreting your statement or exploiting something that just came out wrong, reply to their put-down with something like "I wish I had your quick wit and clarity of expression."

For the person who consistently uses put-downs on you, you should also probably register your disapproval privately and gently with a statement like "I don't like the thoughts that zip through my head when you use put-downs on me. Are you open to relating to each other in a positive way from now on?"

Practice giving sincere affirmations so that it becomes a habit. Almost everyone would rather be in an affirming environment than a caustic one. Wouldn't you?

③ I'm _____; You're _____

Ninety percent of people feel that they're above average.

et's play fill-in-the-blank with "I'm _____; you're _____."
A long time ago people would put mean words in the blanks, such as "bad" or "lost," so that it would read "I'm bad; you're bad." That doesn't make people feel good, does it? So

TIME OUT

The heart is the most deceitful thing there is, and desperately wicked. No one can really know how bad it is! . . . Lord, you alone can heal me, you alone can save, and my praises are for you alone. Jeremiah 17:9-14, TLB.

let's change those mean words and make them nice words!

Let's try the 1970s favorite "OK": "I'm <u>OK</u>; you're <u>OK</u>." There now, doesn't that make you feel a lot better?

That seems to work until somebody who is "OK" does something that others really don't think is "OK," such as stealing or hurting or destroying or even killing. Uh-oh. Now we might *say* "I'm OK; you're OK," but inside we're *thinking* "I'm OK; you're messed up."

And on any given day I might *say* "I'm OK; you're OK," but I will act "I'm OK; you're not." It can quickly get out of hand when I put racial background or socioeconomic status or GPA into the mix. When I'm thinking and acting like that, do you really even want to be around me?

On another day feelings of inferiority may overwhelm me so that even though I *say,* "I'm OK; you're OK," I will feel like "I'm a loser; you're a winner" or "I'm ugly; you're gorgeous," etc.

After several decades of soothing self-talk, it's likely that 90 percent of people feel that they're above average, but the majority have a terribly low self-esteem. (Try the math on that one!) Will more self-help books or daily biofeedback be the answer? Probably not.

It's like the 25 year-old executive who had an embarrassing bed-wetting problem. After the executive had been seeing

In what areas of your life do you need outside help?

a therapist for six months, a friend asked if there had been progress. Quite pleased, the executive reported that things were much better than he had ever dreamed possible. "So, then, you've stopped wetting the bed?" the friend inquired. "Oh, no," replied the executive. "I still wet the bed, but now I'm proud of it." After all, "I'm OK; you're OK."

But in spite of our best cover-ups, busyness, and winsome back-to-nature CDs pumped into our subconscious, the evidence continues to mount: "I'm not OK; and neither are you."

Only when we have acknowledged our need are we able to reach out to the help that is readily available.

 **Willing to Die for It**

What we're really looking for is a life wish.

As a kid I remember hearing stories about martyrs burned at the stake. After the terrifying story someone always seemed to ask, "Would you be willing to die for your faith?" I wasn't sure what faith was, but I knew the dying part didn't sound inviting.

Later I heard about some type of torture in which bamboo pieces get jammed up under one's fingernails. I remembered how painful it felt when my fingernails got trimmed too close. I couldn't imagine trying to live through bamboo being shoved into such a tender spot. That did it. I was convinced that I certainly wouldn't die for my faith.

Some people have creative minds that keep dreaming up new forms of torture. It could be the newest cybervision twist or some ancient, potent version of the rack; merely Russian roulette or having your head held under water by a strong

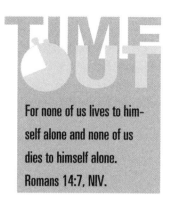

For none of us lives to him-self alone and none of us dies to himself alone.

Romans 14:7, NIV.

hand—whatever the method, I knew I would wimp out.

During my high school years a group of us would get together occasionally for a religious "fearfest." In these settings we would basically share torture stories we had heard or made up and then repeat that haunting question: "Would you recant your faith?" Some vowed to be true, while others wavered. I found myself saying, "Well, you really never know until you actually face it, but I *think* I'd hold out." Inside, I was totally scared to death.

There is a way to find out whether you'd be willing to die for something. It's really quite a simple test. It goes like this: *You'll be willing to die for something if you're willing to live for it.* That's it. Are you willing to live for it? Do you live for it? If so, then you'd die for it too. If you aren't willing to live for it, you certainly wouldn't waste your life by dying for it.

Plug it in. Ask yourself, "Am I willing to die for Jesus?" Then try the other version of the same question: "Am I willing to live for Jesus?" Both answers should be the same. Am I willing to live for Jesus at school? Am I willing to live for Jesus when I'm with my friends . . . all of my friends? Am I willing to live for Jesus where I work? Am I willing to live for Jesus when I'm with my family? Is it possible that I'm willing to live for Jesus in some settings, but not in others?

There's no need for a death wish. What we're really looking for is a life wish. What—or should I say whom—are you willing to live for?

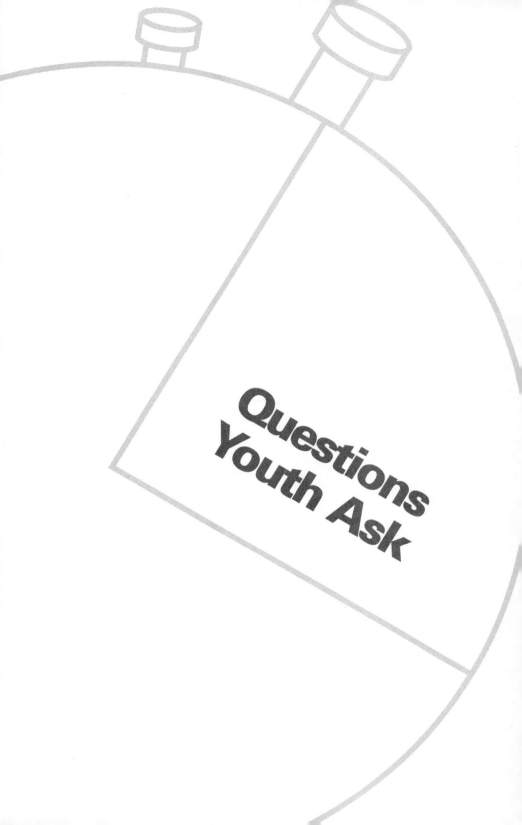

Questions
Youth Ask

What's Wrong With _____?

Let's admit it—sometimes there isn't a very good answer to these questions.

What's wrong with buying a box of staples, putting them through a stapler one crunch at a time, and then swallowing them?

What's wrong with walking around the outside of my house 184 times without stopping?

What's wrong with putting pennies in the offering plate?

What's wrong with taking my meal, putting it in the blender, and then drinking it?

What's wrong with staying up all night if I don't have school or anything the next day?

Perhaps it's a rite of passage in junior high. Actually, for some of us it comes later. I'm talking about the need to question everything. It seems as though our favorite question becomes "What's wrong with _____?" You can fill in the blank with just about anything.

I guess it shows that you won't just accept what somebody else says without deciding if it's worth following. Or maybe it's an authority thing and you just plain don't want to be pushed around.

You might get more of a reaction with such questions as these:

Uh, like, is it wrong to, like, sort of pierce your belly button, like, five times or something?

What's really wrong with ditching school for a day or two?

What's wrong with getting drunk as long as you don't drink and drive?

What's wrong with not going to church anymore?

What's wrong with staying out all night? Don't you trust me?

To actually get in an argument with your parents, a teacher, or some other authority figure may indicate that you're a player in the adult world. Let's admit it—sometimes there isn't a very good answer to these questions. Or if there is a decent answer, the person you're asking might not know it. Maybe they've never asked the question for themselves and you're covering new territory.

But there's another step beyond asking a question that others can't answer very well. A paraphrase of 1 Corinthians 6:12 goes like this: "Just because something is technically legal doesn't mean that it's spiritually appropriate. If I went around doing whatever I thought I could get by with, I'd be a slave to my whims" (Message).

OK, let's say you're old enough to do things totally on your own. Somebody else can't control you anymore. Does that mean you should just go for it? For the immature the answer is obvious—yeah, man! And so, because they're accustomed to being controlled by others, they've never learned how to control themselves. Instead of an authority figure controlling them, their uncontrolled whims or passions dominate them.

There's still another step. There are plenty of things that aren't *wrong,* but maybe there's nothing *right* about them. To answer the question "What's wrong with ____?" might result in a simple "Nothing." But the better question is "What's right with ____?"

Here's my para-

> Just because something is technically legal doesn't mean that it's spiritually appropriate. If I went around doing whatever I thought I could get by with, I'd be a slave to my whims.
> 1 Corinthians 6:12, Message.

phrase of several verses from Galatians 5:

"Let's make it clear—you're free to choose for yourself! The freedom God gives you is the freedom to do good, not the freedom to do what's wrong or just plain wasteful. Here's what all of God's instructions boil down to: love others the way you love yourself."

"Here's a good guideline. Obey the Holy Spirit's instructions. He will tell you where to go and what to do, which is a good voice to hear when you naturally have a selfish streak. You know, we have this natural bent to do the evil things that are just the opposite of the things the Holy Spirit tells us to do. And the good things we want to do when the Spirit has His way with us are just the opposite of what seems to come naturally with us. These two forces inside us are constantly fighting each other, trying to get control over us, and our wishes are never free from their pressures. When the Holy Spirit is alive in your life, you actually don't have to force yourself to do what's right, because the Spirit starts to make that natural in you."

"People who have given their lives to Christ also nailed their natural evil desires to His cross and crucified them there. If we are living now by the Holy Spirit's power, let us follow the Holy Spirit's leading in every part of our lives."

 ## Why Are There No Answers From God?

The Bible is not a recipe book for me simply to grab a few ingredients to stir into my life.

Let's face it—sometimes there just aren't clear answers from God. People say to look in the Bible—they say that the Bible has everything we need. But where do I find which college to attend and whether I should listen to a certain music group (some say they're OK and some say they're not)?

Recently there was a rage for Christian teens to provide a somewhat silent witness by wearing a cloth bracelet with the initials WWJD (What Would Jesus Do?). It also became available in T-shirts, sweatshirts, and probably underwear!

This simple but profound question proved to be the driving force for the characters in a classic Christian novel by Charles Sheldon titled *In His Steps*. Written more than 100 years ago, the book challenged church members to take a vow not to do anything without first asking themselves, *What would Jesus do if He were in my place, having to make the decision I must now make?* Then they were to follow through with what they believed Jesus would do.

Individual lives and entire communities were revolutionized because people chose to live this way. The book is a novel, tragically, because no church has actually lived this way!

At one church where I was a youth pastor, our day camp staff decided to try the pledge for the three summer months. It was voluntary. I joined about half of the staff in taking the pledge not to do anything without first asking myself, "What would Jesus do?" and then, to the best of my understanding and ability, go ahead and do it no matter what the consequences might be.

As a Christian I didn't find it difficult to make the initial commitment. What I did find to be extremely challenging was to discover what Jesus would do! Hebrews 4:15 indicates that Jesus was tempted in all points as we are, but He didn't sin. He can identify with us. But I found it hard to actually comprehend in my life. I read lots of portions of the Bible in an effort to find something that might relate to my

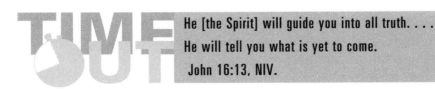

He [the Spirit] will guide you into all truth. . . . He will tell you what is yet to come.
John 16:13, NIV.

current experience and the decisions I had to make. Here are two things I discovered.

1. The Bible is not a recipe book for me simply to grab a few ingredients to stir into my life. I can't just take a verse and plop it into my decision. For example, how should I follow Christ? Jesus told the rich young ruler to sell everything and follow Him (see Luke 18:22). Is that what I should do? But in the very next chapter, another person, Zacchaeus, gave away half of his goods, and Jesus said salvation had come to his house (see Luke 19:8, 9). So which is it—everything or half of everything? And then, in an earlier chapter, a demon-possessed man begged to follow Jesus, but Christ told him to return home and tell others what God had done for him (see Luke 8:38, 39). That makes three very different responses—all from Jesus (and that's just part of one book of the Bible!).

2. Since the Bible isn't a simple answer book (plug in a question and—presto—out comes a ready-made answer), I need the Holy Spirit as a constant source of direction in my life. When He was preparing His disciples for His departure, Jesus told them that the Holy Spirit would be their future source of input. He promised that the Holy Spirit will "guide you into all truth" and "he will tell you what is yet to come" (John 16:13, NIV).

It's not a matter of getting a great road map for life so you can sit down and figure out the exact route you will take. It's more like picking up a passenger who knows the way. The key is to invite Jesus on board first and then to listen to the input He sends your way.

When our day camp plans to use a neighborhood pool fell through we asked, "What would Jesus do?" Some joked that He would walk on water rather than swim anyway. I thought about the time Jesus told the disciples to feed the 5,000—before the miracle took place. I recalled that He sent the disciples out, two by two. I remembered that God came to earth instead of staying removed.

So we went into the community, two by two, and invited people to be part of the day camp. Then we asked if they knew of any pool we could use for the day camp. Before the day ended, many were interested in joining the day camp, and we had a pool we could use free of charge throughout the summer.

Can Someone Who Commits Suicide Still Go to Heaven?

Jesus came to earth on a suicide mission.

I need to answer this more than one way, so stay with me here. Yes, a person can still go to heaven even if they commit suicide, because their salvation depends on Jesus (Acts 4:12), not their decision to commit suicide.

While suicide is tragic and alarming, it's certainly not new. Here are a couple cases from the Bible regarding people who committed suicide. Perhaps an overlooked example is Adam and Eve when they took the forbidden fruit in the Garden of Eden (see Genesis 3:3, 6). That spelled doom for them and for the rest of us, but we can still go to heaven because of the gift of God (see Romans 6:23).

In a sense Jesus came to earth on a suicide mission. While He sometimes withdrew when He saw that people wanted to kill Him (see Matthew 12:14-15), at other times He headed straight back into potential and eventual death (see John 11:8; Luke 9:51). However, He did this in consultation with God, His Father. And because Jesus is God, His death (suicide) brought salvation to all who will receive it. That's a bit different than if you or I were to commit suicide—it doesn't save others.

Samson continues to be the poster child for a person who commits suicide in a seemingly selfish act of final revenge (see Judges 16:28-30). Yet his listing in the "hall of faith" (see Hebrews 11:32) gives us assurance that God's faithful receive heaven by trusting Jesus, not by virtue of their own blameless life record. So *yes,* there are instances in which people who commit suicide will still go to heaven.

> He died for all, that those who live should no longer live for themselves but for him who died for them and was raised again.
> 2 Corinthians 5:15, NIV.

How about another straight answer? *No,* a person won't go to heaven if they commit suicide, and here's why.

Suicide is murder, and the Bible clearly tells us not to murder (see Exodus 20:13). Judas is the poster child for this opposite response to the suicide question. Matthew 27:4, 5 presents a pathetic disciple who has betrayed his master and can't seem to handle it any longer. Although he is pained to the point of acknowledging his sin, there's no indication that Judas accepted a Saviour. And without a Saviour, you won't be in heaven.

And here's the best "straight answer" I can give to the question of whether or not someone who commits suicide will be in heaven: *I don't know.*

Since I'm not God, the answer isn't up to me anyway. If it were, when I'm feeling nice I'd let in a Samson or even a Judas. When I'm not feeling so congenial, I might tell even Jesus that He's not welcome in heaven.

Paul states the obvious: "Sinners don't get heaven, no matter if their sin was a biggie or just the typical everybody's-doing-it kind of sin. And that means you and I don't get heaven. But surprise! By accepting Jesus I get heaven, *and* the Holy Spirit begins living inside of me so that I no longer live a limited, wicked life" (1 Corinthians 6:11, my paraphrase).

And here's an answer to the question you didn't exactly ask, but I read it between the lines: What do I say to someone who's thinking about committing suicide?

When a person is at the end of their rope, feeling overwhelmed with a sense of worthlessness, hopelessness, and lack of purpose, it might be because they finally recognize that life without Jesus really isn't worth anything. They might be ready for a completely new start. This is when 2 Corinthians 5:14-21 really makes sense. Verse 15 reads, "He [Jesus] died for all, so that those who live should no longer live for themselves, but only for him who died and was raised to life for their sake" (TEV). Now, that's a life anyone would want to live.

If you still need counsel on this topic, I'd encourage you to talk with your pastor or another trusted person, maybe using this chapter in the book as a starting point.

Why Bother?

Is there any need to pray since God already knows?

If God already knows everything and really wants what's best for us, then why in the world should we pray? Are we really going to tell Him something He doesn't already know? Are we going to be able to talk Him into something He wasn't already going to do?

These questions are realistic ones, and they demonstrate that a person is wrestling with how powerful and loving God is and just how we fit into the big picture. Are we able to do anything, or are we just to go through the motions while the big boys do their thing?

One of the times Jesus was talking about prayer He said, "Your Father knows what you need before you ask him" (Matthew 6:8, NIV). That one statement makes it sound as if we don't need to ask God for anything, because He already knows everything.

But that's just part of what Jesus said. Let's look at some other things He said about prayer.

A few verses earlier in Matthew 6 Jesus pointed out that those who pray to show off might impress others here on earth, but such "prayers" don't really count in heaven.

Then Jesus referred to the pagan belief and practice that the more times a person repeats a request, the more likely the pagan gods will do something about it. Jesus pointed out that that's not how God is. He explained that we don't have to repeat our prayers to finally get God's attention—God (our Father) knows what we need before we ask Him. He's already focused on us. What a difference compared to the pagan gods!

So back to the initial question—is there any need to pray, since God already knows what we need before we ask?

I think so. Because prayer is about more than requests. It's also about praising and thanking God.

"But doesn't He already know that we're thankful, too?" you might ask.

Let's look at human relationships for some insight on this matter. Don't two people who are crazy about each other already know that? Do they really need to say "I love you"?

Of course the answer is *yes* to both questions. Yes, they know the other person loves them. And yes, they actually need to say "I love you." It's certainly nice to hear it. And it also reinforces the idea in the person *saying* it.

Prayers of praise are music to God's ears, and saying those prayers also reinforces our own admiration of God.

If you need help coming up with prayers of praise and thanksgiving for God, check out some of the following

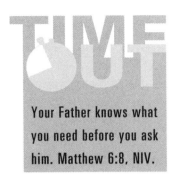

Your Father knows what you need before you ask him. Matthew 6:8, NIV.

psalms: 100, 96, 47, 103, 147, 29, 119, 148, 33, 107, 19, 149, 8, 138, 145, 150, 110, 117, 92, 66, and 111.

Prayer impacts the person who prays. Even psychologists who don't believe in God's existence often acknowledge that prayer benefits their patients. It relieves their anxiety and guilt.

Even Jesus prayed, sometimes spending the entire night in prayer (see Luke 6:12)! Why?

We can get a clue by looking at perhaps the best-known prayer in all of Scripture—the Lord's Prayer (found in Matthew 6:9-13). Jesus begins the Lord's Prayer with the greeting "Our Father," which reminds us that we're God's children. Next He shows us that we should praise God and ask Him for even basic things, such as food.

We should also ask God to forgive our sins, and Jesus presents this with an interesting twist: "Forgive us our debts, *as we* forgive our debtors." To me that means we ask for a heaping dose of forgiveness *so* we can pass it on to others. And while God has made provision for our sins to be forgiven (Jesus has already died), it's clear that we still need to ask for it (see 1 John 1:9).

Another reason we should pray is that our prayers free God to act. Let me explain.

John wrote about a great war in heaven in which Michael (Jesus) and His angels cast out Satan and his evil angels (see Revelation 12:7-9,12). Ever since then Satan has accused God of using His power to bully people around against their will. But God has never done that.

When we pray, we ask God to respond to our requests. Our prayers diminish Satan's power and give God the go-ahead to act in our behalf.

Check out the story about a demon-possessed boy in

Mark 9:29. Notice how Jesus explains to His disciples that prayer is the only way to cast out an evil spirit. In other words, prayer can effectively knock down Satan.

When I think of prayer as a way to free God to stop Satan's harassments, I'm motivated to pray even more. But that doesn't mean I'm informing God of things He's clueless about.

Should you worry about what you say to God in your prayers? No. According to Romans 8:26, 27, the Holy Spirit takes care of interceding for us, rewording our prayers and making them acceptable to God. The important thing is to be saying *something*.

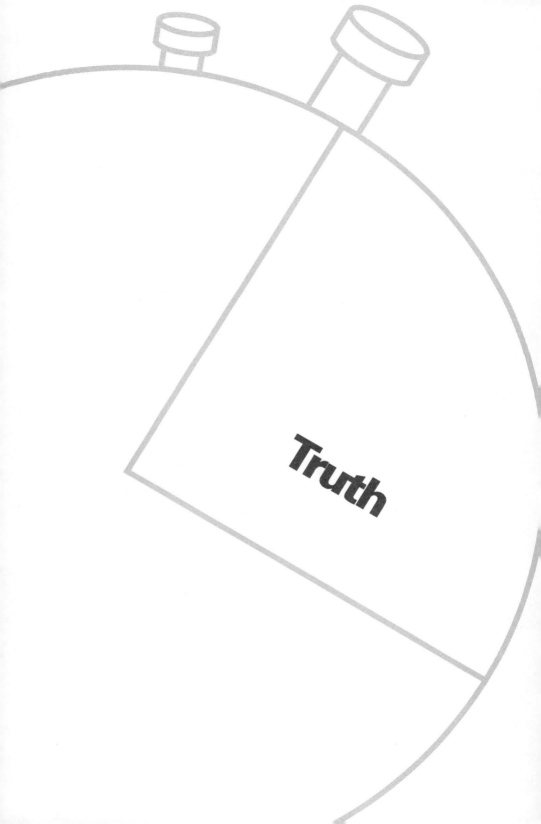

Truth

The God Factor (Reality's Pivot Point)

We recently tried a full century without God.

For centuries people have believed in God, but since belief in God hasn't cured the problems on our planet, we recently tried a full century without God. Unfortunately, this was the century with the most bloodshed of any to date. While Communism promised equality for all, some were always more "equal" than others. Capitalism offered an opportunity for all, but the majority got trampled.

America held that every individual has a "right" to life, liberty, and the pursuit of happiness. In spite of the right to life, abortions are used primarily as birth control. In a land of liberty we can't build enough jails to contain all of our criminals. And our pursuit of happiness keeps us at a frenetic pace with more prescribed and nonprescribed drugs than any nation on the planet.

Beyond these horrific symptoms the problem still remains. If God isn't a factor in life, how do we answer even three of life's basic questions?

1. Where did we come from?
2. Why are we here?
3. Where are we going?

God is the builder of everything. Hebrews 3:4, NIV.

Apart from God, the answers typically are:

1. Slime.
2. Get what you can *or* make the world a *little* better.
3. Who knows? Let's just build on what we have.

Return God to the equation, and the answers look more like:

1. Created by the God of the universe.
2. Live for Jesus.
3. Heaven—and an entirely new start.

You're old enough to transcend beyond merely existing from day to day. When you have a few moments to ask yourself what life is all about, how do you answer the really *big* questions? Either there is a God or there isn't. Which world do you live in?

This Is Huge!

It's a very dangerous prayer.

Perhaps the number one reason friendships end and families fracture is something as basic as forgiveness (actually, a lack of forgiveness).

It probably wouldn't take you very long to think of somebody who has wronged you. Maybe it was talking behind your back, hurting your feelings in a big way, or not being there when you needed that person (and they knew it, too!).

And so you experienced embarrassment, hurt, anger, fear, disappointment, frustration, loneliness, rage, abandonment. In such situations we often think of revenge or some type of payback so the person receives at least a taste of what we experienced. As we replay what happened, inevitably we figure out in our own mind what was behind all of this, which usually just infuriates us more! Where there is no explanation, we create one, and it usually isn't very favorable for the despicable person who wronged us. And it's usually somebody close to us. We rarely get hurt by people we don't know. We simply don't care enough about them to have any expectations or to be hurt by them. It's the ones close to us, the ones who should have cared—they're the ones who can really get to us!

These are the moments when you want to respond to the text: "'Vengeance is Mine, I will repay,' says the Lord" (Romans 12:19, NKJV). You want to say, "Never mind, God; I'll take care of this one for You!" Somewhere between nursing our wounds and plotting revenge, hopefully we allow a moment for God to transform us so that our perspective changes.

One of the elements that make sin so terrible is that the person who sins is also rendered somehow incapable of even asking for the help that is so desperately needed. Instead of coming gently and apologizing, too often there is defensiveness and rationalizing. Sides can be drawn, recruits rallied, and the war is on.

You probably know the Lord's Prayer by heart. But have you really considered what's smack dab in the middle of it? "Forgive us our debts, as we forgive our debtors" (Matthew 6:12, NKJV). Matthew 6:14, 15 clearly states that God will forgive us the same way we forgive others. Let me paraphrase. We're actually praying, "God, I want You to forgive me the same way I forgive others. If I won't forgive them, don't bother to forgive me, OK? If I do forgive someone else, forgive me to the same extent and with the same spirit as I've forgiven others."

Do you really want to pray that? It's a very dangerous prayer! Actually, I want God to forgive me *much more* than

I forgive others. When somebody else wrongs me, I want justice, and I want it *now.* When I wrong somebody else, I want mercy, and please pour it on as soon as possible! How about you?

Others are more gracious than I am, but I've found that I want to forgive only those who haven't done anything very serious. I can overlook a person who steals a dollar from me and at least act as if I forgive him, because I don't care that much about a dollar. But steal $10,000 from me, and I'll call the police to cart you off, and I'll see you in court, and once I get my money back I'll never have contact with you again!

It's finally dawned on me that forgiveness is not something I'm able to come up with. Just as forgiveness is a gift God gives us to draw us back to Him, it's also a gift I need if I'm ever going to give it to somebody else. I simply don't have it on my own, and I can't create it. The best I can do on my own is to put on an act, and most people can see right through it.

The parable of the unforgiving servant (see Matthew 18:23-35) makes it clear that if we accept God's forgiveness, which we certainly don't deserve, we pass it on to others who don't deserve it either. If we don't do that, we don't have the forgiveness that we thought got us off the hook.

If we focus on the wrong somebody has done to us, we'll always have something come between us, and probably both of us will feel justified as we wait for the *other* person to come and apologize. Our focus on the wrong someone has done against us must change to a focus on the forgiveness God has freely given us. With that perspective, either we reject God's forgiveness or else pass it on.

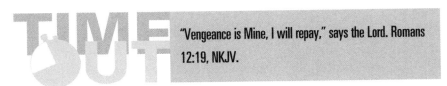

"Vengeance is Mine, I will repay," says the Lord. Romans 12:19, NKJV.

And it's not just a matter of clearing up the wrongs we've done to others. It also includes taking the initiative when someone has wronged us. Jesus pointed out that estrangements must be cleared up before we're even able to worship God (see Matthew 5:23, 24). Imagine it! Somebody has done something against you. That leaves you incapacitated to worship God. And since the person who wronged you probably isn't ready or able to ask forgiveness, Jesus tells us to go and initiate the reconciliation. Then we'll be able to worship Him.

Forgiveness. It's a gift. It's to be received. It's to be given. It brings together what was torn apart. It's the opposite of sin and the antidote to it. And it precedes worship. No wonder this is so *huge*.

Breaking Out of the Box

I didn't know how to act.

Boxes can serve a very useful function. For example, if you have a collection of items that might be too numerous to carry all at once, by placing all of them in a box you can take everything at once. Some boxes are more sturdy than others, and they vary in size as well. A few boxes even have dividers inside of them so the things you carry can be kept in separate compartments.

Life can be relatively simple for most children. As it becomes increasingly complex they might find that their box can't contain everything that's going on in their lives. At this point they must choose whether they will still cram things into an overstuffed box or if they will start to live outside of the box.

As some people move through the education process, their understanding in specific fields may grow exponentially. But that doesn't mean it expands in all areas at the same rate. A person may be brilliant in physics, but be slow in developing relational skills. Another person might do well in mechanical engineering, but still draw stick figures when it comes to art.

I see it frequently with college students who delve into a particular field of study that takes them well beyond the box, but when it comes to their understanding of God, they're still living in a box that would be more appropriate for someone half their age. Perhaps they have forgotten the words God gave Isaiah: "'My thoughts are completely different from yours,' says the Lord. 'And my ways are far beyond anything you could imagine. For just as the heavens are higher than the earth, so are my ways higher than your ways and my thoughts higher than your thoughts'" (Isaiah 55:8, 9, NLT).

The tendency to keep God (or our understanding of God) manageable results in a wimpy or childish God that we're apt to reject or cast aside because, in the words of J. B. Phillips, *Your God Is Too Small* (New York: Macmillan Publishing Company, 1961). Be careful trying to keep God inside a box, because He'll break out, possibly explode out, leaving the box totally useless.

Another potential problem with treating life like a box is the tendency to compartmentalize things instead of integrating them into one complete whole. One of the earliest examples of this is a child acting differently around

> "My thoughts are completely different from yours," says the Lord.
> "And my ways are far beyond anything you could imagine. For just as the heavens are higher than the earth, so are my ways higher than your ways and my thoughts higher than your thoughts."
> Isaiah 55:8, 9, NLT.

their parents than they do around their siblings and friends. I can remember having a certain group of friends at school, another group of friends at church, and still another group in my neighborhood. Without realizing it, I acted different in each setting, sort of fitting in with the way my friends were in that particular arena. I guess you could call me a chameleon.

Life seemed fine in my compartmentalized world, until two of my compartments collided. A few of my friends from school came to my house to play one day. When my "school world" entered my "neighborhood world," I didn't know how to act. Should I act the way I did at school or the way I did in my neighborhood? I remember the tension, the intensity—not knowing how to reconcile my two worlds.

As we continue to move in more circles and interact with more people, we can develop an increasing number of compartments within our box: school, home, work, church, friends, close friends, sports, Saturday night personae, etc. I've found that most teens can identify with 20 to 30 different compartments within the box called their world. Perhaps if Jesus would ask us who we are, our true response might be more like the demoniac who said, "I don't have one name; I have many names because we are many" (Mark 5:9, Clear Word).

So not only does God break out of any box we might try to put Him in, but *we* need to break out of the box we make for ourselves. You can press the issue yourself by having different compartments of your life intersect, such as hanging with your school friends and your work friends together, or involving your church friends in a service project in your neighborhood. Take your parents with you some Saturday night and see how you (and they) act!

The process of becoming an integrated person can be lengthy, embarrassing, and even painful. But it's the consistent and true way to live. The alternative is the life of a demoniac.

 **Toolmaster**

How can you know if money is your tool or your master?

Money is the root of all evil!" the preacher rebuked. "You cannot serve both God and money. That's why God gives you the opportunity to put it in the offering plate."

From the way the preacher dressed and the junk heap he drove, just about everyone in the congregation felt rich in comparison. Not wanting to be evil, they gave and gave and gave.

But the preacher went too far when he indicated that he would have to retire in Costa Rica, where the few dollars he had been able to save would stretch far enough for him to survive. One church member took the liberty to fly to Costa Rica. The preacher's dollars must have really stretched far, because he had a mansion overlooking the sea, complete with servants.

Before you jump all over the misleading preacher, let's make an important correction in his first text. The Bible does not say that money is the root of all evil, even though many people think that's what it says. According to 1 Timothy 6:10, "For the love of money is a root of all kinds of evil" (NIV).

Is there really any difference between "money" and "the love of money" being the root of all kinds of evil? Most definitely! If "money" is the root, then rich people are the evil ones. And most of us don't consider ourselves to be rich, so the verse wouldn't apply to us. How convenient!

If "the love of money" is the root of all kinds of evil, then everyone, no matter how much money they have or don't have, is susceptible to evil to the extent that they love money. It's possible to be very poor and still love money (materialism, things, etc.). And it's possible to be rich and *not* love money.

The stereotype labels rich people as miserable in spite of

their money (or because of it) and poor people as saints close to God. Just for the record, I've met rich people who were very happy and poor people who seemed to be the opposite of saintly. Here is where contentment supersedes money. If you lack contentment, you'll probably desire more.

> The love of money is a root of all kinds of evil. 1 Timothy 6:10, NIV.

Throughout my life I have been at various stages of the American middle class. I have always been able to point to scores of people who have more than I. But on mission trips to poor villages in other countries I feel like a millionaire, and I am in comparison. I make commitments to live in poverty or at least to give more to others. Then I return home and find myself sliding back into wanting more. I'm a middle-class American, and I love money. I keep finding the root of all kinds of evil being replanted in the soil of my life. How about you?

Money itself is only a tool. It's not good or evil in and of itself. It can be used for either. It's like a car following a bank robbery and shoot-out. A car can be used for the robbers' getaway, or it could be used to take a wounded victim to the hospital. The car isn't good or evil; it's merely a tool. The same could be said about money.

So money is a tool for us to master rather than it being a tool that masters us.

How can you know if money is your tool or your master? "Where your treasure is, there your heart will be also" (Matthew 6:21, NIV). What's most important to you? God? Friends? School? Clothes? Nintendo? Sports? Computers? Music? Missions?

Make a list and then prioritize the items: number one, number two, and so on. Then compare what percentage of your money gets spent on the various items on your list. If you don't have much money, what percentage of your time is spent on these items?

Here's what's really amazing. Your "investments" can change radically through a significant event like a mission trip, a convicting sermon or testimony, a conversion experience, etc. Where you put your resources indicates what's really important to you. Here's how that same text, Matthew 6:21, reads in some other versions:

"Your heart will always be where your riches are" (TEV).

"It's obvious, isn't it? The place where your treasure is, is the place you will most want to be, and end up being" (Message)

"If your profits are in heaven your heart will be there too" (TLB).

Money is a tool. Is the tool your master or are you the master of the tool?

Life
Experiences

Into My Heart

*At some point in your life you must deal with
whether or not Jesus will be your God.*

I grew up in a Christian home, attended church each week, and even went to a Christian school. But just because a person grows up with those advantages doesn't make the person a Christian. When I was in third grade, people called me "Jesus' boy." But by the time I reached junior high, I had shed that image. I wasn't a bad kid, just unconverted. The God stuff seemed fine for adults and for kids, but I was too cool to be interested in it.

When I was a high school freshman it seemed that my purpose in life was to make the older students feel macho by picking on me. My high-and-mighty self-image got dragged in the dust quite a few times, even though this was supposedly a Christian school. Once the entire school took a one-week retreat to the coast. Later I found out it was primarily for a spiritual time of revival, though we also had some outdoor classes. At the time all that mattered to me was that we didn't have school and that we got to play a lot.

But something very strange happened. A bunch of the students went through this conversion experience. Lots of people were crying and giving testimonies. Even though many of my friends joined in, I kept my distance. It was tough, but I managed to make it through the entire week without getting converted.

After we got back to school things were different. My friends would come up to me and ask, "What did you read in the Word this morning?" I didn't know we had an assignment. When they invited me to a prayer group after lunch I wondered if we were having a surprise test and needed emergency prayers. "No," they would respond, "we just want to pray." I couldn't relate. It seemed real to them, but foreign to me.

One weekend my friends invited me to join them for an afternoon in the park to sing and pray. I didn't really want to, but there was nothing else to do, so I joined them. We sat in a circle on the grass and sang a bunch of songs. Then they started to pray. Most of the prayers were for other students not present—that they would somehow find the Lord. I was glad I was there so they wouldn't pray about me.

Then, across the circle from me, my sister—the one just a grade ahead of me, the one whom I always fought with, the one who had already joined this mass conversion thing—started praying for me . . . out loud. "O Lord, please do something to reach my brother. I know he has a hard heart. But You can work a miracle. Please do that so that he can be saved."

I couldn't believe it. Out loud, right in front of everybody. I wanted to go over and smack her one. But then I realized that would demonstrate how great my need really was. So I kept silent and determined to pay her back once we got home.

When she finished, one of my friends started to pray. "Lord, she's right. Steve is lost. But we believe You can save him. You know what a big ego he has. But please save him in spite of himself."

They're ganging up on me! I thought. One after another people in the circle prayed for me.

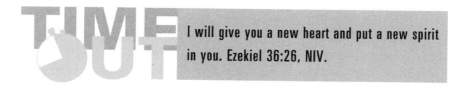

I will give you a new heart and put a new spirit in you. Ezekiel 36:26, NIV.

I believe that there's a cosmic battle between good and evil, between Christ and Satan. But this mega-showdown happens inside each person's heart, too. And it was happening inside of me as they prayed. It felt like a high-tension tug-of-war. I felt myself being pulled toward Christ, back to Satan, then to Christ. Finally I said, "That's it; I quit! I'm in!"

Everybody in the group started whooping and hollering, "It's a miracle!" they said. "If God can save Steve, He can save anybody!"

I didn't feel jubilation; I felt peace. The war was over; the battle had ended. For the first time in my life I chose Jesus for myself. I had been able to say "No" to Him, and now I said, "Yes." The result was peace.

Joy pounced on me about a half hour later. Then I was jumping up and down and shouting, "Hallelujah! Praise Jesus."

I'm not saying it has to be that way for everybody. That's just the way it was for me. But at some point in your life you must deal with whether or not Jesus will be your God.

There's a saying that goes like this: God has no grandchildren. In other words, you can be a child of God, but you can't be a grandchild of God. Your parents being children of God doesn't make you a grandchild of God. God has no grandchildren, only children.

If you've grown up on your mom's spiritual apron strings or your father's spiritual shirttail, it's time for you to grow up for yourself. Is Jesus real to you? It's time to go direct. By now you're certainly old enough for Jesus to come into your heart.

As a child you may have sung that childhood song "Into My Heart." Have you sung it for yourself lately? Are you ready to do so now?

2 Can't You Accept a Gift?

I do even more than my part.

The summer began with such promise. I would be selling Christian books and could earn enough to pay for an entire year of college, possibly more. During the training session I sold an entire set of books during one of the breaks. What would happen when I went door-to-door for an entire day?

As it turned out, not much. Even though I considered God fortunate to have me selling books for Him, nobody would buy. Others in the group also had a difficult time, but at least they sold a few items. The area director came and spent half a day just with me—for support and to give a few pointers. Together we sold nothing. He spent the second half of the day rotating among the other salespeople. Each person he spent time with started selling more books. I stood out as the jinxed person.

Then the regional director came and spent an entire day with me. We forged a plan: When potential customers wouldn't go for the expensive hardback books, we would pull out a cheap paperback version and sell it for a buck or two, just to get some spending money for food and gas. We had one woman pinned into the corner of her house. We promised to leave as soon as she purchased just one book. She stiffened and refused. We went for the paperback for $2. "No." We countered with an offer of only $1. Still "No." We dropped the price to 35 cents, promising to head directly out the door after we received a quarter and a dime. "No!" We left without any sale.

For lunch we stopped at a local grocery store and purchased

a couple bagels and cream cheese. The total came to $3.76, which I quickly calculated to be less than $2 for each of us. The regional director was on a salary and made the purchase.

But I'm not a freeloader. I do my part, carry my own weight; no handouts for me! In fact, I do even more than my part. I offered him a full $2. He refused. But I wouldn't be turned away. When he wouldn't take the two greenbacks, I dropped them on his lap when he sat in the car. He returned them to my lap. I countered by stuffing them into the ashtray and held it closed.

Without fighting, he firmly grasped my wrist and asked, "Can't you accept a gift?" The rest of my world seemed suspended as the question reverberated through my consciousness. "Can't you accept a gift?" God's offer of the gift of salvation flashed across my mind. "Can't you accept a gift?" Inaudibly I answered, "No!" And if I couldn't accept a mere $2, there was absolutely no way I had accepted God's huge gift of salvation.

The question and its implications haunted me for several days. It humbled me to the point of giving up on my visions of greatness, which freed me to accept all that God has to give me. Instead of keeping score, I now bask in the tremendous gift(s) God has given me. I can now accept gifts from others, too.

As far as the summer of selling books went, I barely made enough money to get started back in college the next year. But it was one of

If, by the trespass of the one man, death reigned through that one man, how much more will those who receive God's abundant provision of grace and of the gift of righteousness reign in life through the one man, Jesus Christ. Romans 5:17, NIV.

the best summers of my life. After all, what could be better than fully embracing God's gift of salvation?

Can you accept a gift?

 ## Go With the Flow

I should have gotten a clue from nature.

It's a fact of nature. I had heard about it before. But it actually happened inside of me.

At age 14 I experienced a new-birth type of conversion. The moment is one I'll always remember. Peace flooded my soul, followed by overwhelming joy. I felt like I was on a spiritual high for months! A bunch of us who had been part of this revival met together regularly to pray and study Scripture. It kept us alive.

But gradually the feeling started to die. I could sense it leaving. Eventually we stopped meeting together. We still went to church, but it lacked the vitality from before. We got into discussions, but they were more head trips than heart calls. Spiritually, we died.

I don't remember anyone ever saying it, but somehow it got into my head that if I read two chapters of my Bible each night, I could be spiritually resuscitated and even maintain that emotional high that had been lost.

So I did it! With commitment and fortitude I read two chapters of my Bible each night before I went to bed. And I was faithful! Throughout an entire year I missed maybe three or four nights. I was good! Admittedly there were some nights when I couldn't tell you anything I had read immediately after my ritual. And there were a few nights when I found myself asleep with my face in my open Bible—I had literally fallen asleep while reading my two chapters. But I stuck with it. And I continued to be as dead and dry as parched sand during a drought.

I should have gotten a clue from nature. The Jordan River empties into the Sea of Galilee. That's the sea full of fish, especially if you put your nets on the right side of the boat. It's the sea that can have seemingly instant storms. Pigs ran into it and people dove into it and Jesus scared and calmed people by walking on it. The Sea of Galilee is alive.

The Jordan River not only empties into the Sea of Galilee, but it also continues out the other side. The Jordan River feeds the Sea of Galilee, but the Sea of Galilee also feeds the Jordan River, which continues south through Palestine and eventually winds up in what is called the Dead Sea. Quite a tourist spot, the sea is below sea level and has no outlet, and the resulting salinity makes it very easy to float while swimming. Though it's fed with fresh water, it ends up being salt water because it has no outlet. Therefore, it doesn't have much life in it.

The Jordan River feeds both the Sea of Galilee and the Dead Sea. The difference is that the Sea of Galilee has an outlet, but the Dead Sea doesn't.

That described my life. I had lots of input—two chapters of Scripture each night, a Bible class five days a week at a Christian school, additional religious instruction at church each week, a Christian family. But I had no outlet. Input with no outlet results in a dead sea. For me it resulted in a dead spirituality.

After more than a year of deadness, the stalemate ended when I was put in front of a church to

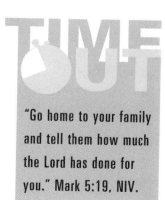

"Go home to your family and tell them how much the Lord has done for you." Mark 5:19, NIV.

preach. The strung-together clichés I uttered made me sick. The listeners graciously showered me with kind comments, but that night, while faithfully reading my two chapters in the Bible, I sought a message from God to share with others. This was different from just going through the motions of reading two chapters. The Bible became alive. My Dead Sea became the Sea of Galilee. I finally had output to match my input. I became spiritually alive again.

What's it like for you? Do you have an outlet to share spiritually? If not, I doubt if you're spiritually alive.

On the other hand, some people are good at output, but they don't have much spiritual input. Their spirituality goes dry because they lack input. Where are you getting your spiritual input?

It's a simple fact of nature. You need input and you need output. Where are you getting it? Where are you giving it? To be spiritually alive, you've gotta "go with the flow."

 ## Unsportsmanlike Conduct

I found that I reacted the same way off the court as I did on the court.

Are you blind? I can't believe you missed that!"
It was my first season of intramural basketball. Our school didn't participate in interscholastic sports at the time, so my budding career that would take me to the NBA started in a small gym.

With a flash of skill (and luck) during the first game of the season, I had people talking in surprised tones about this little freshman. I was ready to live up to a reputation much bigger than I could deliver.

And that's why, when I drove the lane and got fouled,

I couldn't believe the official didn't call it. I missed the shot! I wouldn't ever miss a layup unless I had been fouled. Wasn't that obvious by now? But the blind zebra with the whistle in his mouth didn't make a sound, and the opposing team already had moved the ball to the other end of the court while I whined in disbelief.

Later in the game I drove the lane and wasn't fouled, but I still missed the layup. So I went through the same antics. After all, if the official didn't see me get fouled, he probably didn't see me *not* get fouled either. It was important that any potentially adoring fan be assured that I hadn't lost my touch (luck) and that I was being abused by everyone on the floor, including the officials.

The next time I missed a shot (I can't remember if I was actually fouled or not) and disgustedly passed the blame to the officials, they finally blew their whistles, but it was to call a technical foul on me! Can you believe it? I'm the one who (probably) got fouled, and they penalized me. Out of a sense of justice (and to try to make myself not look so foolish) I protested . . . and protested. That's when they gave me a second technical. And that meant I was kicked out of the game.

It seemed to me like a clear-cut case of conspiracy. But my imaginary fans didn't come to my rescue. The officials certainly weren't about to. The opposing team seemed pleased that the crybaby was gone. My own teammates physically escorted me from the basketball court so they could continue the game without me.

Before I could play in the next game the following week, I had to apologize to the officials and promise not to lose control again. Although I wanted to ask that the officials at least be given seeing-eye dogs, I held my peace because I wanted to play.

Of course they missed the fouls again. And I lost my temper again. And I received a technical foul again. And again. And so I was removed from the gym a second time. How could I stay on my path to the NBA when I kept getting ejected from these little intramural games?

The physical education teacher wasn't sure what to do with me. Finally he decided that I couldn't play again until I had officiated at a game. I jumped at the opportunity! I'd show them how to do it right!

To my dismay, I found out that sometimes other players blocked my view of what was happening. Sometimes the angle wasn't right to know for sure whether contact was made. And then some of the players had the audacity to complain that I was missing the most obvious calls. I compensated by calling some fouls that really weren't fouls. Suddenly I wished that I weren't wearing the black-and-white-striped shirt with that lousy whistle around my neck.

They say it's an Indian proverb: "Don't criticize a man until you've walked in his moccasins." For me, it became "Don't criticize an official until you've officiated." What a change it made in my perspective! I now knew what it was like outside of my little world.

Just think, God moved into our world and knows exactly what it's like to be in our shoes. "This High Priest of ours understands our weaknesses, for he faced all of the same temptations we do, yet he did not sin. So let us come boldly to the throne of our gracious God. There we

> This High Priest of ours understands our weaknesses, for he faced all of the same temptations we do, yet he did not sin. So let us come boldly to the throne of our gracious God. There we will receive his mercy, and we will find grace to help us when we need it. Hebrews 4:15, 16, NLT.

will receive his mercy, and we will find grace to help us when we need it" (Hebrews 4:15, 16, NLT).

As a bonus insight I discovered that sports provides a microcosm of life. I found that I reacted the same way off the court as I did on the court. The difference was that it tended to happen faster on the court. If I could learn how to live life on the court in a game that really didn't matter all that much, I could transfer that to the bigger game of life.

Paul said it this way: "All good athletes train hard. They do it for a gold medal that tarnishes and fades. You're after one that's gold eternally. I don't know about you, but I'm running hard for the finish line. I'm giving it everything I've got. No sloppy living for me! I'm staying alert and in top condition. I'm not going to get caught napping, telling everyone else all about it and then missing out myself" (1 Corinthians 9:25-27, Message).

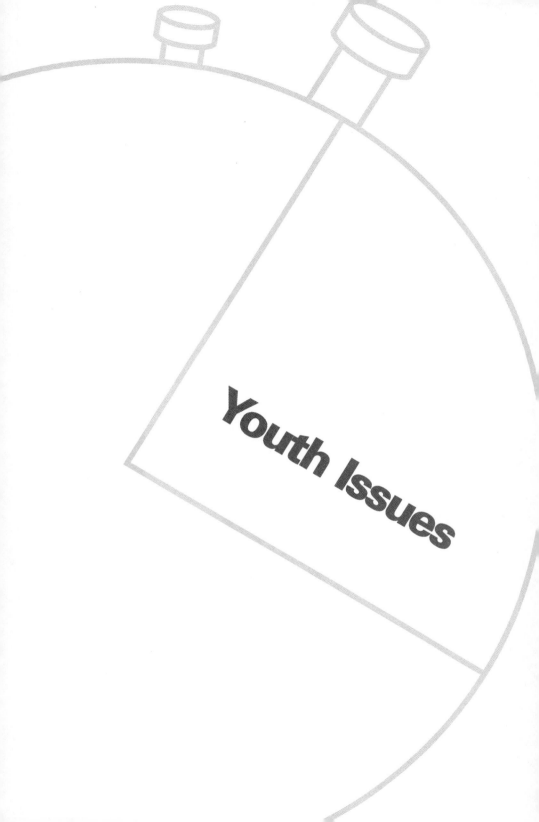

Youth Issues

1 Not Good

At some point you must come to terms with your sexuality.

At the close of each day of creation, God surveyed what He'd made and pronounced it "good." The one exception came when He created male and female of every animal but humans. The creation of Adam was "not good" (see Genesis 2:18) until God created Eve, thereby making God the original matchmaker.

Over the centuries the tension and celebration of the male and female relationship and interactions have created sorrow and joy well beyond words. In my own lifetime I've seen the pendulum swing from total equality for optimum androgyny on one extreme to a "Mars and Venus" differentiation on the other extreme.

When in the company of only one gender, it might be safe to share gender jokes. But it's rarely wise to try it in mixed company.

For example, why did God create Eve after He created Adam?

Female response: Artists like to make a rough draft before they create the real thing.

Male response: God didn't want to hear a bunch of suggestions on how He should make Adam.

By the way, what's the difference between males and females?

A man will pay $2 for a $1 item he wants. A woman will pay $1 for a $2 item that she doesn't want.

A woman marries a man expecting he will change, but he doesn't. A man marries a woman expecting that she won't change, but she does.

It's probably best to not go any further. In fact, it probably would have been better if I had not gone there at all.

When it comes to males and females, one thing for certain is that the full image of God, the image in which we were created, the thing that sets us apart from all of the rest of creation, is not complete as male; nor is it complete as female. This is not to say that people are incomplete unless they are hooked up with the opposite sex. It simply reveals that the image of God cannot be contained in only one gender. "So God created man in his own image, in the image of God he created him; male and female he created them" (Genesis 1:27, NIV).

The celebration of the image of our Creator-God reaches the ultimate through sexual intercourse. But in our culture, sex has become a game, a performance, a one-night stand, a trophy to brag about, an experiment, a way to say "Hello" or "Goodbye," and it's not good. We have allowed Hollywood to shape our expectation that within 60 seconds of a magical glance between a man and a woman, there is certain to be a cutaway to a bedroom scene with the sheets up to the waist of the male and just covering the breasts of the female.

In contrast, God's intention is to develop a male-female romantic relationship over time so that the celebration of sexual intercourse has many steps along the way. In the 1980s Donald Joy's *Bonding: Relationships in the Image of God* (Waco, Tex.: Word Books, 1985) presented 12 steps in the physical coming together that too often gets reduced to merely sex. The first three steps don't even involve physical touch, but instead have to do with what is visual.

It's possible to have a tremen-

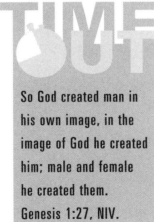

So God created man in his own image, in the image of God he created him; male and female he created them.
Genesis 1:27, NIV.

dous thrill by holding hands, but by too many people's standards, that's far too tame to really count for them, which is *not good*. By racing toward intercourse, people lose the many steps of exhilaration along the way. Instead of gleefully celebrating each step, intercourse has become the goal, and ironically, performance becomes the evaluation tool, even though the full experience has been short-changed.

It's like eating a cake that has baked for only five minutes instead of 30. It's like eating a pear before it's even started to ripen. It's like attempting to appreciate an oil painting that has only its first color on the canvas. It's like expecting to drive cross country when you only took time to put one gallon of gas in the tank. It's simply *not good*.

God's intention for sex is that it will draw two people together to the point of "cleaving" (Genesis 2:24, KJV). The word "cleave" gets translated as join, unite, and cling in different versions. It can be illustrated by gluing two pieces of paper together so that they permanently bond. In fact, if you try to separate them after they "cleave," both pieces of paper will be horribly damaged in the process. God's intention is that people who cleave together will stay together. Simply having sex denigrates God's design for us to the realm of animals in heat, which is *not good* for those created in the image of God.

One major step to get out of our culture's promotion of sexual prematurity is postponing or staying out of the dating game. Josh Harris's *I Kissed Dating Goodbye* (Sisters, Oreg.: Multnomah, 1997) presents one model of this.

At some point you must come to terms with your sexuality. God created it as something extremely good. No wonder Satan has made it a major focus to turn it into something *not good*. Contrary to what some young people think, our God-given sexual drive is not something simply to hold back on until we get married or something we do whenever we feel like doing it. It's all the steps of celebrating a developed and lasting relationship in the image of God. And this gift is not just for the adolescent years. It's for the rest of our lives. And that is *very good.*

Fill 'er Up

Alcoholic spirits are a cheap substitute for the real Spirit.

Years ago gas stations had employees who actually pumped the gas for you. As you drove into the station, an employee would quickly come to the driver's side and ask, "Fill 'er up?" This somewhat rhetorical question suggested that you wanted to purchase a full tank of gas, and they would oblige. If you were a teen, you'd most likely respond by saying something like "No, just $5 worth" or "Well, it looks like it will be only $2 today" or "Can I just get 37 cents' worth and we'll see how far I can go?"

These days we're quite accustomed to self-serve gas stations. If we hear the words "Fill 'er up" we're more apt to think of something for us to drink rather than putting gas into a vehicle. And when we think of drinking, it's most likely alcohol.

The fact is, many teens drink in order to get drunk. Some estimate that as many as 50 percent of high school students in the U.S. attend drinking parties at least once a month, and half of these (one fourth of all high school students) get "bombed" (very drunk) at least once a month. Depending on whom you talk to, it may seem like "everyone's doing it." I've talked to a number of high school students who don't drink. They often hang with other nondrinking students, so they don't feel like everybody's doing it.

Why do people drink? It's the "in" or hip thing to do. It's highly social in the American culture. Some drink to relax, to fit in, to escape, to celebrate, to experiment, to be macho, to remove pain or inhibitions, to loosen up, or to be the life of the party. Some even imbibe for religious or sacramental reasons.

A 1988 study of Adventists in the United States revealed that alcohol use increased the younger a person was. Of those age 65 or more, only 5 percent used wine at least once in the previous month. Of those age 44 to 65, 10 percent used it. Of those age 30 to 43, 20 percent used it. And of those age 18 to 29, 25 percent used wine at least once the previous month. In this particular study, no survey data was available for high school students. We would expect it to be high. We do know that in the general population, an alcohol-related auto accident is the leading cause of death for 15- to 24-year-olds.

Some people drink for the potential euphoria that lies somewhere around a blood alcohol level (BAL) of .05—which is somewhere between one and three drinks, depending on your size and several other factors. Others drink specifically to get drunk—to leave their current consciousness and enter a different one.

Here's the irony and the tragedy. The benefits people associate with drinking alcohol are available through the Holy Spirit, and they come without the negative side effects. Paul put it this way: "Do not be drunk with wine, which will ruin you, but be filled with the Spirit" (Ephesians 5:18, NCV). In other words, alcoholic spirits are a cheap substitute for the real Spirit.

When you drink deeply of the real Spirit, you'll be free of inhibitions and free to celebrate. With the Spirit, you can escape the entanglement of sin. Your security from the Spirit frees you to be what God intended you to be from the start. One main difference is that you'll

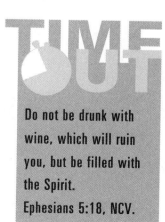

Do not be drunk with wine, which will ruin you, but be filled with the Spirit.
Ephesians 5:18, NCV.

actually be aware of it when it happens and will remember it the next day too. Instead of putting yourself and others at risk, it puts all of you at a great advantage. After all, you want the real thing, the Spirit, rather than the cheap substitutes, the spirits.

 # A Blueprint for Your Life

Go ahead and make a choice.

God has a specific plan for your life!"
Hey, isn't that great? The God of the universe has mapped out every step of your existence. Aren't you special? Don't you feel cared for and totally supported?

Initially it packed me full of assurance and pumped up my confidence meter. My life was set—God would now move me through the motions.

Should I wear jeans or khakis? pierce that body part or not? go on a mission trip or save that money to attend a Christian college? Should I even go to college? If so, which one? And what about marriage—have I met that ideal person yet, the one God picked out just for me?

In time that feeling of being cared for changed to feelings of isolation, neglect, and desperation. What did God want me to do next? Why didn't He communicate?

I tried getting instructions out of the Bible, but where does it tell me which socks to wear or which major to declare when I sign up for college classes? Should I work in the courts of a king, as Daniel did, or lead people out of an established nation, as Moses did? Or should I dump everything, as Peter and Andrew did, and follow Jesus? If I did that, where would I go and what would I do?

I listened for that "still small voice," but only heard my

own weighing of what appeared to be equally good options. What would tip the scales so I would know what God's specific plan was for my life? I wanted to follow it. The problem was that I couldn't find it! Why couldn't I hear God's instruction, as Abraham did? If God told me to go to Nineveh, I wouldn't run away, as Jonah did. My futile attempts to hear or sense God's guidance led me to a most discouraging conclusion: I must be so distant from God that I can't hear him screaming out His plan for my life.

After years of frustration and repeated guesses at what God's plan for my life might be in big areas as well as small ones, my expectations got completely revamped when a friend shared with me a book, *Decision Making and the Will of God.* In the Bible we read about God's direct messages to prophets, but Daniel didn't receive visions every day. What other cities did Jonah get sent to besides Nineveh? Abraham's first recorded contact from God came at age 75! And according to the biblical stories, there were years, even decades, between some of God's messages to him.

This doesn't mean that God isn't involved in our daily lives, whether it's knowing the number of hairs on our head, intervening to spare our lives, bringing a word of encouragement as we cross paths with certain people, or opening the door for new areas of service. It simply means that when God sends a specific directive for my life, it's exceptional rather than something I should expect each day like marching orders from my military commander.

Perhaps what sets us apart from the rest of God's creation is the God-given brain with which we can think and make rational choices. Instead

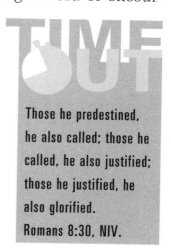

Those he predestined, he also called; those he called, he also justified; those he justified, he also glorified.
Romans 8:30, NIV.

of irresponsibly waiting for God to make decisions He has equipped you to make, go ahead and make a choice. Remain open for God to send specific instructions, but don't expect it, because He hasn't ever given people such information for every step they have taken.

But God has provided a broad stroke of His will for each one of His children. According to Romans 8:30, we have been predestined by God to become more and more like Jesus. Now, there's a blueprint that's flexible enough for all and yet specific enough to provide the needed guidance. And it's available every day.

 # When?

Some yearn for a more sensational story.

You wouldn't believe how bad I was! All the sex—sometimes three or four different women the same night, and that doesn't include the times it was group sex. The booze and drugs—deadly combinations that took me out of my mind to the point that I don't remember anything that happened some of those nights. It's a miracle that I'm alive today. But I do remember joining the gang and the first five times that I killed somebody. After that I quit keeping track of how many I knocked off.

But then I met Jesus! And everything in my life of sin came to an end. He gave me a new life, hallelujah! I'm a completely different person now. I was saved, converted. I was going one direction, and now I'm going the opposite direction. And you need to do the same thing.

Really?

Maybe. Maybe not.

Have you been converted? When?

The majority of people who grow up in a Christian home

can't name a specific time or place for their conversion. They can't recall that on March 16, 1998, while rock climbing with two friends, they slipped and knew they would plunge to their death, but their belt loop caught on a slight lip. They gasped, "Oh, God," and then they heard a voice out of nowhere say, "Yes, I've been here all along. Now I want you to start living for Me." Nope, there's no Damascus Road experience for them.

If a conversion is a complete change in a person's life, a new birth, a new creation, an about-face, is that what's truly needed? What if you grew up loving Jesus, attending church faithfully, living a life in which you sometimes struggled with various temptations, but never lost your hold on Jesus? Would doing an about-face and heading the opposite direction take you toward Jesus when you're already headed that direction?

When I talk about conversion with young people who have grown up in the church they frequently say something like "It was sometime during seventh grade . . . or maybe it was eighth grade . . . or it could have been . . . I'm not really sure, but it was sometime around then. Anyway, it just seemed like God was more real in my life. When I read my Bible and prayed, it seemed like things were alive. I did that kind of thing before, but it started being more personal. I don't know, I guess that's about it."

Some yearn for a more sensational story. A few feel that they need to immerse themselves in the world and then come back to Jesus so they can have a "real" conversion story. Then they'll have a specific answer when someone asks them, "When did you become a Christian?"

How pathetic! Perhaps some have to go over fool's hill in order to one day come to their senses, but I haven't met a single

I have been crucified with Christ and I no longer live, but Christ lives in me. Galatians 2:20, NIV.

person who was glad they tried out the world before trying Jesus. But I often hear them say they wish they would have come to Jesus sooner.

Perhaps when a person desires a specific time and place to label their conversion, what they really want is an awareness of the reality of God through some type of supernatural experience. If you can't label a specific time or event in which Jesus became real to you, here are some ways to become aware of it.

1. Journal God's activities in your life over time.
2. Put yourself on the line for Jesus by doing street ministry.
3. Go on a short-term mission trip.
4. Participate in a prayer conference.
5. Become friends with someone dying of AIDS.
6. Pray, pray, pray.
7. Try leading two different people to Jesus.

For some people, life is relatively flat and uneventful. But maintaining the status quo wasn't the way Jesus lived. And He never called His followers to be so passive. So if you want God to be more real in your life, start putting yourself more on the line—to the point that you really need Him. I'm not talking about being recklessly presumptuous like jumping off a cliff and asking God to somehow save you. I'm talking about taking the risk of looking foolish and potentially becoming a laughingstock unless God steps in.

Read Matthew, Mark, Luke, and John. When you feel that you have a sense of what Jesus was about and how He responded to various situations, transfer that to today and start living the way Jesus did. When you do that, the stories from Acts will also start to happen in your life. And instead of wondering "When was I converted?" you'll have difficulty remembering when Jesus wasn't real to you.

Core Beliefs

Beyond the Shadow of a Doubt

You don't have to wonder, to guess, to hope.
You can know.

Perhaps it was my perfectionistic bent. Maybe the challenge of trying out various identities during adolescence left me wondering what would stick and what wouldn't in my life. Whatever the cause, I found myself struggling over and over and over during my teen years with that basic Baptist question, "Are you saved?"

My answer varied, depending on my mood, who asked, what I was doing at the time, and who was around to hear my response. Am I saved?

"Yes, at least I think so."

"No, and nobody knows for sure."

"I hope I am."

"If you think you are, then you probably aren't. If you think you aren't, then you probably are. So I don't think I am saved (because I *do* want to be saved)."

"It's presumptuous even to consider that question!"

The first time somebody shared the text with me, it must have passed right over my head. "God has given us eternal life, and this life is in his Son" (1 John 5:11, NIV). It sounds like any preacher. God is the one who gives eternal life through Jesus. But how can a person really know that they have it?

The very next verse provides simple algebra that even a legalist can comprehend. "He who has the Son has life; he who does not have the Son of God does not have life" (verse 12, NIV). There it is—the deciding factor: the Son. Here's my paraphrase. "If you have Jesus, you've got it. If you don't have Jesus, it's simple—you don't have eternal life." For those who aren't sure whether or not they have Jesus, just take a moment to invite him into your heart. Zappo, now you have Him regardless of whether He was or wasn't there before.

I have no idea how many times I came to that point and then thought, *It can't be that easy; you really can't know for sure.* I'm convinced that's why John included the very next verse: "I write these things to you who believe in the name of the Son of God so that you may know that you have eternal life" (verse 13, NIV).

You may know! You don't have to wonder, to guess, to hope. You can know! So when the devil would harass me about being secure with God—what others call "the assurance of salvation"—I would take another trip, slowly, over those three verses in 1 John 5:11-13. You could check out any one of my many Bibles and find those verses underlined, sometimes with special notes added in the margin.

So how do you answer the question "Are you saved?" Beyond a memorized, pat answer, what is your response at the foundation of your heart? Because *you can know!* Instead of wavering between the "saved, not saved" uncertainty, ask the question a second way: "Do you have Jesus?" The answer to that question can be inserted for the first one. And if you have any question about whether or not you have Jesus, ask Him to come into your life right now.

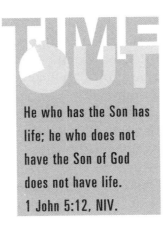

He who has the Son has life; he who does not have the Son of God does not have life.
1 John 5:12, NIV.

Jesus, sometimes I wonder if I'm saved or lost. There are times I feel truly saved. Other times I feel totally lost. And then there are those in-between times of not knowing. So I'm clinging to the words You gave me in 1 John 5:11-13—that eternal life is based on having Jesus. Thank You for making it that simple. I'm not going to play the little game about whether or not I have Jesus. Right now I just ask You to come into my life completely. I know You won't say no to that request. And that means I have the Son, which also means I have eternal life. And if there's any question, I need only to remember that You made it a promise— I can know that I have eternal life. Thank You, Jesus. Amen!

 **Tricky**

We are God's poetry.

As a child matures, one of the typical developments is some sort of sense of justice—what's fair and what's not fair. It can be a little tricky. After all, each person seems to come up with their own unique brand of justice, often one that tilts in their favor most of the time.

One of the general principles is a sense of equality in which good gets rewarded and bad gets punished. Parents get plenty of opportunities to implement this procedure. Those who neglect these teachable moments might not get many more chances through their neglectful parenthood years.

Frequently God gets brought into the process: Jesus is happy when we are good and sad when we're bad. For some reason, the lyrics "Jesus loves me when I'm good/when I do the things I should" get repeated. But the rest of that verse, "Jesus loves me when I'm bad/even though it makes Him sad," rarely finds root in our recall machinery. Bible stories of God's judgments seem more easily recalled than narratives of God's mercy.

When somebody attempts to share the concept of grace with us, it's difficult to accept, so we make it more complicated, since it doesn't fit our beliefs about fairness. Why would God give us something for nothing? How/when can we repay Him if He really is giving it to us? There's got to be some sort of payback necessary, probably with interest.

God saved you by his special favor when you believed. And you can't take credit for this; it is a gift from God. Salvation is not a reward for the good things we have done, so none of us can boast about it.

Ephesians 2:8, 9, NLT.

The homogenized statement from the committee goes something like: "Your good works don't save you, but if you are saved, then the good works must follow. If they don't, then you really aren't saved." There may be some theological truth in the statement, but you can almost feel the tone of "You'd better be good, or else . . ." Then comes the reminder from some form of James 2:17 that faith without works is dead.

A biblical example could be the parable of the sheep and goats found in Matthew 25:31-46. Those who do the good works go to heaven and those who fail to do them get the fires of hell along with the devil and his angels. What most people overlook is that the "good guys" weren't even aware that these good works counted.

For centuries many have found it difficult to figure out a satisfactory relationship between salvation and good works (or "faith and works," as some would say). If the salvation side received too much emphasis, it seemed that God was handing out gifts indiscriminately and so freely that the gift must have held little real value. Some referred to it as "cheap grace," meaning that it cost the receiver nothing and therefore was valued as such. When the good works side received too much emphasis, it seemed that either a person could never do enough good deeds to merit salvation or else they achieved it and really didn't need a Saviour.

Ephesians 2:8-10 presents the full picture and provides a surprise regarding the relationship between salvation and good works. In the *New Living Translation* it reads, "God saved you by his special favor when you believed. And you can't take credit for this; it is a gift from God. Salvation is not a reward for the good things we have done, so none of us can boast about it" (verses 8, 9). (That presents the salvation part pretty clearly, doesn't it? Now, here's the tricky twist on the good works side of the equation in verse 10: "For we are God's masterpiece. He has created us anew in Christ Jesus, so that we can do the good things he planned for us long ago."

The word translated "masterpiece" is the word poiēma, from which we get the English word "poem." In other words, we are God's poetry. He is creating poetry with our lives once we accept His salvation. In fact, He has already worked out the first draft long ago. He's just waiting for us to say "Yes" to salvation so He can then make our lives a masterpiece.

So good works are not a way in which we balance the ledger sheet by paying back God for His gift of salvation. Good works are a gift from God *in addition* to the salvation He gives. *Both are gifts from God.* So release the record-keeping and celebrate both gifts—salvation and the poetry God is now writing with your life!

Perhaps one of the ways we lose sight of this is by expecting God to write the identical poem in each life. We think that the behaviors of each person should be in lockstep with everyone else in order to be approved. Let the poet create His poetry. After all, He already planned it out for us long ago. It doesn't have to be so tricky.

Holiday or Holy Day?

The Sabbath actually is the symbol of trusting completely in God for your salvation.

The very first full day any humans had on this planet was a Sabbath (see Genesis 2:1-3). But who needs a sabbatical rest when you're just getting started? Evidently humans do! God made it for us, not for Himself.

And the purpose of the Sabbath, for starters, is to get with God. When you start with God and spend significant time with Him, the rest of the world falls into place. And that was true even before sin became part of the human equation (again, refer back to Genesis 2:1-3).

Fast-forward to God's people being delivered from hundreds of years of Egyptian slavery. Time for a sabbatical? God takes them to Sinai for a new orientation for their new life. He institutes yearly religious festivals. But He tells the people to "remember" something they no doubt had forgotten—a full day each week with a special focus and intimacy with the One who created them and saved them from slavery (compare Exodus 20:8-11 with Deuteronomy 5:12-15). It's time to remember!

Fast-forward again to Jesus worshiping on Sabbath thousands of years

> There remains, then, a Sabbath rest for the people of God; for anyone who enters God's rest also rests from his own work, just a God did from his.
>
> Hebrews 4:9, 10, NIV.

after Creation. Evidently God's people are remembering, at least in form. How appropriate that Jesus picked a Sabbath to announce the purpose of His mission—to set people free! (See Luke 4:16-21, which includes a quote from Isaiah 61:1, 2.) Remember that God not only made you and redeems you from the slavery others may put you in, God also frees you from slavery to sin and sets you free! Remember. In fact, every week take a sabbatical and get your bearings straight.

There's absolutely no indication from Scripture that God wants us to forget this. And for those tempted to think that Sabbath is all about following the Ten Commandments, go deeper and discover that the Sabbath actually is the symbol of trusting completely in God for your salvation, a rest from any attempt to work your way to heaven (see Hebrews 4:9, 10).

Fast-forward once more to right now. The idea of taking a sabbatical each week strikes most as a day "off" rather than a day "on." Our orientation makes the workweek the primary focus with a day off to recuperate. We often think that's what holidays are for. But the Sabbath is our "on" day, the purpose or focus for the whole week.

In a technical sense, the primary meaning of "holiday" is a holy day, a day set aside to commemorate a holy event. That seems appropriate for Sabbath, especially since it's all about God and us being together. But its secondary meaning has probably become our primary meaning—it's a vacation, a chance to chill, to veg out, to just relax and do nothing. That puts Sabbath in a category more like leftovers.

Perhaps looking at it relationally will resonate with our time warp lifestyle. If you're stuck with people you don't want to be with for more than 10 minutes, it seems like days; if you're stuck with them for a full day, you start to understand what the term "eternity" means! But if you're with a person who makes your heart flutter, a day seems like a millisecond. When you want to catch up with a friend that you never seem to spend enough time with, a full day together becomes the highlight of your week.

When God makes an appointment to spend a full day with you each week, what's it like for you—a holiday or a holy day?

Remember.

Mega-Star Wars

When winning doesn't seem possible, refer to the end of the story.

Were you into the *Star Wars* stories? How about *Star Trek*? Some were (are?) totally consumed by it. Several people have shared with me how these paralleled the story of the great showdown in the universe between Christ and Satan.

Perhaps it's because I'm not a science fiction person, but I haven't seen these certain classics. As others have shared with me the story lines, I must agree that some elements do seem remarkably similar to what some have called "the great controversy." But some parts don't seem to match at all.

Storywriters, English literature professors, playwrights, dramatists, TV writers, and others know that the basic plot is a simple three-step process of a situation, complication, and resolution. In a TV situation comedy the opening scene will present the situation and a complication. That's intended to hold your interest for the rest of the program. In fact, before each commercial, another complication will be presented to entice you to stay tuned so that you can be led to resolution.

The specifics of the story don't matter as long as the writer follows this three-step process. Old Western movies of cowboys and Indians featured the process every bit as much as *Star Wars* later did. You'll find it in cartoons, James Bond movies, and romantic comedies. The same is true of stories in book form. All good stories captivate you and then hold your interest through a conflict between the good guys and the bad guys.

There might be cues, such as a white horse or a friendly look or good deed, to point out the good guys. It's the good guys who get into a bind that seems pretty much impossible to get out of, even though you really want them to. Bad guys often appear in dark colors, have monstrous looks, and can destroy anything until it comes to really finishing off the good guys.

The tension of good and bad gets played out in war, sports contests, and even academic achievement. Wherever competition exists you will find the potential for a tension that will spark interest and a desire for resolution. Even if you feel assured that the good guys will win, sometimes it just doesn't seem possible.

The Bible has many great stories—stories with a situation, complication, and resolution; stories with a tension between the good guys and the bad guys. The first book of the Bible presents God's creation of a perfect world (see Genesis 1-2). The complication is that the serpent deceives Eve and Adam, which will destroy them and hand the perfect earth to the devil (see Genesis 3). In this tension, it looks like the bad guys will win. But with a dramatic flurry of surprises, the Creator becomes the Redeemer both of humans and of the new heavens and new earth (see Revelation 21:1-4).

The second book of the Bible, Exodus, chronicles a series of plots with tension between the good guys and the bad guys. Moses should have been killed with the many other Israelite babies, but God provided a way out. He's in line to rule Egypt,

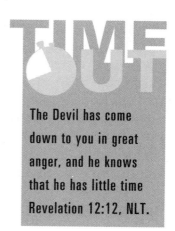

The Devil has come down to you in great anger, and he knows that he has little time Revelation 12:12, NLT.

but then has to flee to Midian. He returns with the power of Yahweh, but Pharaoh repeatedly opposes him. After the Israelites finally leave Egypt, Pharaoh pursues them into the Red Sea, where he meets his end. But the rest of the book presents a host of additional complications and resolutions.

You'll find additional plots throughout Scripture, especially in the last book of the Bible. In Revelation 12:7-9 we read about a story that actually precedes the first book in the Bible. "Then there was war in heaven. Michael and the angels under his command fought the dragon and his angels. And the dragon lost the battle and was forced out of heaven. This great dragon—the ancient serpent called the Devil, or Satan, the one deceiving the whole world—was thrown down to the earth with all his angels" (verses 7-9, NLT). Good news for heaven, but not for earth. A few verses later we read, "Terror will come on the earth and the sea. For the Devil has come down to you in great anger, and he knows that he has little time" (verse 12, NLT).

It's not surprising that in Revelation 6:10 those who have been martyred cry out to God, "How long will it be before you judge the people who belong to this world for what they have done to us?" (NLT). But the last two verses of the entire Bible contain a promise that God will return soon, and He offers His grace to hold us through until then. And *Star Wars* is nothing compared to the true cosmic showdown!

The same story gets played out in individual lives too. In your life there are certain to be some complications. Perhaps a resolution doesn't seem possible. It may appear that all hope is gone and the bad guys will actually win. But according to the story, God does win. So when winning doesn't seem possible, refer to the end of the story. It may be just the thing you need to face the complications in your life during this mega-star war.

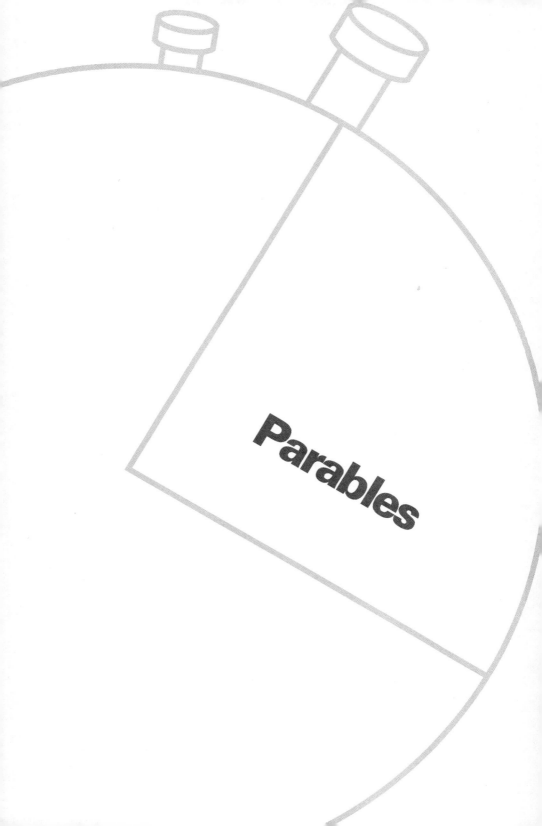

Parables

Parables

Compu-Gig

A lot of good anything new would be.

At last—no more mooching off others or going to the computer lab at school; no need to wait around until the people at Mom's office are done so I can finally get a chance to use their computer. I was finally going to have my own computer!

I found out firsthand what people mean when they say "You get what you pay for." An old family friend actually gave me the computer. He may as well have given it to a museum. Did you know that at one time they actually made computers without hard drives? What was that all about? And the disk slot was thin but wide, if that's possible. They said it used 5¼ disks. What's a 5¼ disk? So you could say that I had a computer—kind of. But it was worthless.

So I went ahead and invested some actual cash into a computer. No, it wasn't the latest with all the bells and whistles. It wasn't that fast. But at least it worked and it used regular disks. And, yes, it had a hard drive—I made sure of that! Since it was used, or shall I say "preowned," it came with some software already installed on it—pretty lucky, huh? I was excited. I stayed up late that first night, just playing the games already on it. I even typed a report for one of my classes. This was great! By the second week I purchased a new game and then got the shock of my life. There was no more space on the hard drive! A lot of good anything new would be. It's sort of embarrassing to admit it, but there wasn't even one gigabyte of memory on the hard drive. I guess I got scorched on that one.

So I was faced with dumping what I have on the hard

drive just to get something new. There's no way that would cut it. Either I needed to get a new hard drive and go with additional peripherals or else get a real computer.

I went for the real computer, one with gigabytes (plural!). It even had an internal modem, standard. So I got on the Internet and started e-mailing all kinds of people, including a bunch I'd never heard of or met before. It was a real kick. Isn't it amazing how it's sometimes easier to talk to or write to a total stranger than it is to talk with those close to you? Weird! But that's what I did. Talk about sleeping with the enemy! I'm not even sure where it came from, but one of those e-mails not only choked me up, it choked me out! I got a virus. Not AIDS; the computer kind. But it was killing my computer, which was killing me! It was a nice computer . . . while it lasted . . . until that stupid virus came and choked it out!

OK, you get what you pay for. So I paid. Dearly! I had searched around quite a bit and had read up on what's out there. You want memory? Try 88.6 gigabytes! And speed? We're getting close to 1,000 megahertz now! And no more surfing the Net—it's more like blitzing! I can run any program and can do it quickly! I have built-in virus protection. I should have done it this way from the start. It has to do with really being ready.

> The one who received the seed that fell on good soil is the man who hears the word and understands it. He produces a crop.
> Matthew 13:23, NIV.

And it was just as true for a farmer planting his seeds in Jesus' day. Check out that story in Matthew 13 or just listen to this story again to catch the analogies.

Runners Needed

*Just being around those guys made me feel like a
real runner.*

They say it's good for you. I'm not fanatical or anything,
but I decided to check into it. And you know what?
They're right! I'm talking about running. Now, it's always
possible to overdo even a good thing, but with a commitment to moderation, I got into running.

The most important item is your running shoes. Trust
me, you don't want those antiquated ones. Today there are
literally hundreds to choose from, with probably more than
one type tailored specifically for you. I shopped around
until I found some I really liked. They looked good, but,
more important, they felt good. I paid a good amount, but
sometimes you just have to make an investment if you really care about something.

Every week or two I'd visit what had become my favorite
running store. Their salespeople were top of the line,
trained and experienced in running with the credentials to
prove it. They're the ones who invited me to a seminar in
which they took a liquid foam impression of my foot, took
anthropomorphic measurements, videotaped me in a wind
tunnel, and then scanned all of that into a computer until
they came up with the perfect shoes made just for me. Just
being around those guys made me feel like a real runner.

Each time I went to the running store I got more and more
involved. Did I mention that those guys are experts at mar-
keting, too? One time I found out about a running magazine,
so I subscribed. Another time I found out that my regular
sports socks are pretty worthless compared to the no-wicky-
no-wefty, fiberfill, hyperlightomatic, airflow socks. I bought

two pairs to alternate for my training runs and another pair just for races.

Did I mention the races? I found out about a bunch of them right at the running store. In fact, I even went to a few and cheered for the runners. They were great! And they did look healthy! I noticed that most of them had special shirts and running shorts. So I asked for more information back at the running store the next time I dropped by.

What I hadn't realized was that because of different weather conditions, I really needed several running outfits—one for regular weather and another one for hot days. Of course, to be a year-round runner, you have to have a different outfit for those cool mornings, and I even purchased one for very cold weather. I didn't buy the running suit with reflectors and battery-powered night lights. Remember, I made a commitment to be moderate—not really a fanatic.

At a running expo I found out about carb-loading, super-energy bars, and little packets of gooey nutrients for those really long runs. They had free samples of the super-nodule mineral drinks that taste horrible but are essential for serious runners. I also got a special belt with movable, lightweight, Velcro water-holders because I heard you can really get dehydrated when you run and they say, "It's all downhill after that!"

So have I started running? No, not yet. I'm not fanatical, you know.

I do not run like a man running aimlessly; . . . No, I beat my body and make it my slave so that after I have preached to others, I myself will not be disqualified for the prize.
1 Corinthians 9:26, 27, NIV.

"Ready or Not, Here I Come"

It's as though they're deaf to the "Ready or not, here I come" warning.

Most kids have played the game hide-and-seek. You really need only two people to play, but the more the merrier! One person closes their eyes and counts to 20 or 50 or 100 (depending on how fast the person counts and if they know how to count all the way to 100) while everyone else scatters and hides.

When the counter reaches that magical finish number, the shout goes out: "Ready or not, here I come." At that point there's no excuse for not being hidden. Usually the counting is even done aloud so others can hear and know how close they are to the beginning of the search.

I've lost count of how many times I've played the game. But I'm still shocked to notice that some people are still scurrying around when the announcement "Ready or not, here I come" sounds across the playing area. I can't help wondering if they've ever played the game before or if they are so indecisive that they really can't find a place to hide.

Inevitably there's at least one person who keeps changing hiding places. To start, the person may have tried following another person, only to discover that the hiding place worked for only one person, not two. Then there might have been a search for other fellow-hiders, followed by superficial hiding places, demonstrating that this person certainly hasn't hidden on their own before. Becoming repeatedly aware that the current hiding spot probably isn't very good, another is sought, sometimes rather blindly. Such a person may or may not be caught in motion once the counting ceases. It's a daring place to be. Onlookers feel nervous for the skittish hider.

Of course, another category of players knows exactly where to hide the instant the counting commences. Usually familiar with the area, perhaps hosting the game, such people typically are well hidden by the time the counter is only at the halfway point. Because they know such great hiding places, others may try to join them. The reception varies, depending on the space available, whether or not the first person is friendly, and how well newcomers might fit in. But ironically, if those already hidden speak out to shoo away others who want to join them in such a wonderful location, the noise they make could expose them, provided the counter is listening for telltale sounds.

Then there are those caught completely unaware that the counter even completed counting. You wonder why they are so surprised when they get discovered, usually wandering about in the open. It's as though they're deaf to the "Ready or not, here I come" warning. Sometimes they protest about how unfair things are, or perhaps that the counter didn't shout loud enough. They'd never say something like "You know, I just wasn't listening, was I?" They often drop out of the game after one or two rounds.

Occasionally you'll get a couple of talkers. Their hiding place may be fairly decent, but they can't seem to be quiet or stay still. They give themselves away by their noise and/or unnecessary movement. But usually they don't mind, because they figure they won't be alone as losers—they have somebody with them. That's what the game is all about to them anyway.

He who testifies to these things says, "Yes, I am coming soon." Amen. Come, Lord Jesus.
Revelation 22:20, NIV.

And some don't even listen to the counting. They say they want to play, but there seems to be no indication that they are actually playing. They may wander aimlessly or even strike up a brief conversation with the person counting. You wonder if they really know how to play, or if they just say that they do. You know that when the call goes out, "Ready or not, here I come," they won't be ready.

When Jesus comes, all kinds of people will be in varying stages of readiness. It's not a matter of a hiding from Him; it's a matter of being ready when He arrives. The sooner you find your place, the less you will fear those words. In fact, you can actually be eager to hear, "Ready or not, here I come!"

Oh, My God!

It's really hard to fully explain it; you just have to experience it.

Even though many have made it a high priority on weekends, the majority probably still aren't fans. Why, they wouldn't know the difference between a Dolphin and a Ram. And if they did, you know they wouldn't have a clue who the players are, at least the current ones. Face it: Most people aren't true fans.

Besides knowing their teams, true fans can name their favorite players. And they willingly pay excessive prices to purchase their jersey along with the team logo on a ball cap. Season tickets separate the truly loyal from the wannabes and mere talkers. The actual location in the stadium isn't nearly as crucial as simply having season tickets.

Of course, nothing gets in the way of game day. True fans prepare 24 hours in advance—usually with plenty of food and drink. Diehards arrive way before the opening kickoff. They find just being in the stadium to be practically a spiritual experience! It's really hard to fully explain it; you just have to experience it.

Outside of game day, there are always other team events available. Players show up for various community events to autograph paraphernalia and actually talk to the fans. It's pretty awesome. Some of them are giants. Others are very down-to-earth and almost like you, except they're a lot faster and certainly more famous.

Did you know that you can get a tattoo of your team right on your arm? It's not that expensive. Of course, you have to know that you want to be affiliated with that team and not just one or two of the players. I mean, the players might move, but the team will always be there promi-nently displayed on your arm. I suppose it could be re-moved (like all tattoos), but that would be painful. Besides, having it sort of tells everyone who you are and what you think about that team.

Because people move or die or just lose interest, teams are always seeking to add to their fan base. Sometimes you'll come across people actually trying to get you to switch to their team. The one thing I'll never understand is people who aren't fans at all. Can you believe it? They're ac-tually going through life oblivious to real living. You've got to wonder if they have any meaning in their empty lives.

> For I resolved to know nothing while I was with you except Jesus Christ and him crucified.
> 1 Corinthians 2:2, NIV.

I was talking to one the other day. He said that for every activity I de-scribed about sports, he could find a counter experience in his passion. Without realizing I just gasped, "Oh, my God!"

And he said, "Exactly!"